PRAYERS
FOR THE SEASONS
OF GOD'S PEOPLE

PRAYERS
FOR THE SEASONS
OF GOD'S PEOPLE

Worship Aids for the Revised
Common Lectionary, Year A

B. David Hostetter

ABINGDON PRESS
Nashville

Cataloging-in-publication information applied for with the Library of Congress

ISBN 0-687-33749-6

98 99 00 01 02 03 04 05 06 07— 10 9 8 7 6 5 4 3 2 1

MANUFACTURED IN THE UNITED STATES OF AMERICA

Contents

Preface 7

Advent/Christmas

First Sunday of Advent 9
Second Sunday of Advent 12
Third Sunday of Advent 16
Fourth Sunday of Advent 20
Christmas Eve/Day
(First Proper A, B, C) 24
First Sunday after Christmas Day 27
Second Sunday after Christmas Day 31

Epiphany

First Sunday after the Epiphany
(Baptism of Our Lord) 36
Second Sunday after the Epiphany 39
Third Sunday after the Epiphany 44
Fourth Sunday after the Epiphany 47
Fifth Sunday after the Epiphany 50
Sixth Sunday after the Epiphany 54
Seventh Sunday after the Epiphany 58
Transfiguration 61

Lent

First Sunday in Lent 66
Second Sunday in Lent 69
Third Sunday in Lent 73
Fourth Sunday in Lent 76
Fifth Sunday in Lent 79
Sixth Sunday in Lent 82

Easter

Easter 88
Second Sunday of Easter 91
Third Sunday of Easter 95
Fourth Sunday of Easter 98

Fifth Sunday of Easter 102
Sixth Sunday of Easter 105
Seventh Sunday of Easter 109
Pentecost 112

After Pentecost

Trinity Sunday 118
Proper 4 (May 29 - June 4) 121
Proper 5 (June 5-11) 125
Proper 6 (June 12-18) 128
Proper 7 (June 19-25) 132
Proper 8 (June 26 - July 2) 135
Proper 9 (July 3-9) 138
Proper 10 (July 10-16) 142
Proper 11 (July 17-23) 145
Proper 12 (July 24-30) 149
Proper 13 (July 31 - August 6) 152
Proper 14 (August 7 - 13) 156
Proper 15 (August 14 - 20) 159
Proper 16 (August 21 - 27) 163
Proper 17 (August 28 - September 3) 166
Proper 18 (September 4 - 10) 170
Proper 19 (September 11-17) 173
Proper 20 (September 18-24) 177
Proper 21 (September 25 - October 1) 180
Proper 22 (October 2-8) 184
Proper 23 (October 9-15) 187
Proper 24 (October 16-22) 191
Proper 25 (October 23-29) 194
Proper 26 (October 30 - November 5) 198
All Saints (November 1
or First Sunday in November) 201
Proper 27 (November 6-12) 204
Proper 28 (November 13-19) 208
Christ The King - Proper 29 (November 20-26) 211

Scripture Index 216

Preface

When I served as a pastor in the Presbyterian Church in Canada, I frequently used James Ferguson's *Prayers for Common Worship* (London: Allen & Co., 1956). Particularly as a pastor faced with the task of leading morning and evening services for a number of years, I often turned with appreciation to Ferguson's book, which began with the following inscription:

Morning and Evening
Every Lord's Day
Throughout the Course
Of the Christian Year

With the use of newer translations of the Bible, I found it necessary to update the language of my public as well as my private prayers. Thus began the composition of a collection of prayers geared to the Revised Common Lectionary which I have used in my own ministry. Using Ferguson's book as a guide, I have now completed this annual cycle of prayers of invocation, confession, thanksgiving, dedication, intercession, commemoration, and prayers of the day, and have included one-sentence introductions to the lessons for the day. Having used them weekly for some time myself, I offer them here in the hope that other pastors and leaders in Christian worship will find them of benefit.

B. David Hostetter

Advent/Christmas

First Sunday of Advent

First Lesson - The prophet urges God to make a dramatic entrance into the world and impress the nations. Isaiah 64:1-9

Psalm 80:1-7, 17-19

Second Lesson - This is the beginning of Paul's first letter to the church at Corinth. 1 Corinthians 1:3-9

Gospel - Jesus alerts the disciples in apocalyptic terms of the coming of the Son of Man in clouds of glory. Mark 13:24-37

CALL TO WORSHIP

Leader:The grace of our Lord Jesus Christ be with you all.

People:And also with you.

Leader:Wait expectantly for our Lord Jesus Christ to reveal himself. He will keep you firm to the end, without reproach on the Day of our Lord Jesus.

People:It is God in Person, who called us to share in the life of the Son, Jesus Christ our Lord; and God keeps faith.

INVOCATION

Eternal God, we wait upon you at this time, alerting ourselves to watch also for the currents of history, the rivers of time that roll on, generation after generation. We come especially to give thanks that your Son Jesus came among us to share our life so that we might share yours. Your Spirit inspires our prayers, in the name of Jesus, our Savior. Amen

PRAYER OF CONFESSION

God of many names, by what name shall we call to you? Our question rises out of some confusion, not only about who you are, but about who we are, for you have declared yourself to be our kin, One who has ransomed us. In some ways you are like a permissive parent, who allows us enough room to get ourselves into trouble when we follow undisciplined instincts. Too often we are more like people who claim no affinity to you than like a people who bear your name. Forgive our tendency to slough off responsibility for our decision. Excuse the incompleteness of many of our confessions. We trust you still because of Jesus Christ, your Son. Amen

Declaration of Pardon

Pastor: Friends, hear the Good News! God has given you grace and peace in Christ Jesus

People: and enriched us with many good gifts.

Pastor: Friends, believe the Good News!

People: In Jesus Christ, we are forgiven.

[AND]

Exhortation

Be alert and watchful, for no one knows when the Son of Man will come with great power and glory. Do not neglect to finish the work he has given you to do.

PRAYER OF THE DAY

Divine Timekeeper, keep us alert by the chimes of the times that whether Christ comes again, at dawn or high noon, in the evening or at midnight, we will be ready to welcome his return, enabled by the Spirit to show that our house is in order and that we are honored by his coming. Amen

PRAYER OF THANKSGIVING

God of grace, Child of peace, Spirit of truth, we join with all the members of the church everywhere in the world in giving thanks for all the gifts you have given to enrich the whole church. Though each of us does not have all gifts, there is no needful gift lacking to your church through the talents you have distributed among us. In Jesus Christ you have given us life and truth, grace and peace. Through days of persecution and days of plenty, you have sustained the church and kept it firm in expectation of the return of the Lord, Jesus Christ. Your favor is unmerited. Your peace is undeserved. Your truth is beyond our comprehension. We celebrate your generosity, in Jesus Christ. Amen

PRAYER OF DEDICATION

Lord of the church, you are not enriched by our gifts but enable us to share our talents for the enrichment of the whole congregation, young and old and middle aged. We present ourselves to be useful to each other and to you. Amen

PRAYER OF INTERCESSION
AND COMMEMORATION

God of the ages, from ages past no one has heard, no ear has perceived, no eye has seen anyone besides you, who works for those who wait for him. You meet those who gladly do right, those who remember you in your ways. You are concerned not only about us in our own neighborhood but all the nations of the world and every locale. Though you are the Creator who may destroy what you have made like a potter with a pot that is imperfect, you reshape human societies in expectation of a more perfect vessel. Continue to speak to the nations through the scriptures and the church that there may be a new heaven and new earth redeemed from rebellion and violence.

As we approach another Christmas and listen for the angelic anthem of peace on earth, grant the world not only the traditional "cease fires" that often suspend armed conflict at the season but a spirit of reconciliation that should be the approach of the church of Christ. May the church in every nation preach the apostolic message: "Grace to you and peace from God our Father and the Lord Jesus Christ . . . "

Strengthen and purify the church so that it may be blameless on the day of our Lord Jesus Christ.

By your power, great God, our Lord Jesus healed the sick, giving new hope to the hopeless. Though we cannot command or possess your power, we pray for those who want to be healed. Close wounds, cure sickness, make the broken whole again, so that the ill may be well and happy in newness of life. Help us to welcome every healing as a sign that, though death is against us, you are for us, and have promised renewed and risen life in Jesus Christ the Lord.

In the coming of Jesus of Nazareth, Invisible God, you have let your face shine on us so that we may be saved. We rejoice in the salvation of all who from the beginning have put their trust in your grace and been received into glory. Enrich us in the testimony of Christ, so that we are not lacking in any spiritual gift as we wait for the new revealing of our Lord Jesus Christ or in death we are taken to be with him. To our Lord Jesus, to our faithful God, to your ever present Holy Spirit, we ascribe all grace and peace, time without end. Amen

Second Sunday of Advent

First Lesson - The prophet advocates smoothing the way for the coming of God like a just and caring Shepherd. Isaiah 40:1-11

Psalm 72:1-7, 18-19

Second Lesson - Peter reaffirms the declaration of Jesus that the time of the second coming is a surprise but that the upheaval will bring justice and peace. 2 Peter 3:8-15*a*

Gospel - The beginning of Mark's gospel connects the ministry of Jesus with the prophecy of Isaiah and identifies John the Baptist as the forerunner of Jesus Christ. Mark 1:1-8

CALL TO WORSHIP

Leader:The grace of our Lord Jesus Christ be with you all.

People:And also with you.

Leader:Hear the words of the Lord. Are they not words of peace, peace to God's people?

People:We hear the words of our Lord Jesus to us, his loyal servants, and to all who turn and trust in him.

INVOCATION

Holy God, we come to worship you, to confess that we believe you to be just and merciful. You send us the Prince of Peace to lead us in paths of peace. Lead us by your Spirit that we may follow him always. Amen

PRAYER OF CONFESSION

God of the first day, God of today, God of the last day, we admit that we are more frightened by the threat of a nuclear accident or a nuclear war than we are hopeful for a new heaven and earth. It is like our apprehension of major surgery, an unpleasant experience, but one that can bring about the condition in which healing can take place. We may be fatalistic and feel powerless to change unjust institutions that provoke and promote war. Forgive our reluctance to look for the new day and to work for justice and peace with patience, repentance, and perseverance, whatever the disappointments and delays. Baptize us with the Holy Spirit according to the gospel of Jesus Christ, your Son. Amen

Declaration of Pardon

Pastor: Friends, hear the Good News! God has forgiven
your guilt

People: and put away all our sins.

Pastor: Friends, believe the Good News!

People: In Jesus Christ, we are forgiven.

[AND]

Exhortation

Prepare a road for the Lord through the barren places of our
common life. Clear a highway for God across the fruitless
areas of our history.

PRAYER OF THE DAY

Jesus Christ, Son of God, since you have walked in our shoes,
enable us by the same Holy Spirit of our baptism to proclaim
the good news and prepare the way for your coming again
so that you may be surrounded by people from all earth's
cities and countrysides. Amen

PRAYER OF THANKSGIVING

Saving God, loving Christ, baptizing Spirit, hear our thanksgiving for all who have paved the way for your good news
to reach us. We admire the bold preaching of the prophets
and apostles. We appreciate the work of scholars and trans-
lators in preparing a written text for us to read. We are grateful
for the printers and binders who make Bibles for us and for
all who help us to read and understand the Word of God
written. Most of all we thank you that your saving and
forgiving love was embodied in Jesus of Nazareth, the great
Good Shepherd who has gathered his flock into the church.
For past deliverance, for present comfort, for future promise,
we give you thanks, faithful God. Amen

PRAYER OF DEDICATION

We worship you, loving and faithful Lord, by the presentation of these tokens of our prosperity and the yield of our work. Use us and our offerings to spread the gospel of Jesus Christ. Amen

PRAYER OF INTERCESSION
AND COMMEMORATION

Comfort your people, O God, not only in Jerusalem, torn with racial and religious tensions, but inner cities of the world, which are so often the scene of poverty and prostitution and violence against persons and property.

Sustain the voices of repentance and new life in the inner city and in every moral wilderness, to prepare the way of the LORD and help the lost to find a highway to God and a better life. Reveal the glory of the Christ Child again in the rough places of human pain and poverty.

While the church waits for the second coming of Christ and a new heaven and earth, may we strive to be found by him at peace, without spot or blemish, and using the time of your patience to preach the good news of salvation by word and work.

Faithful God: you have power to set us free from harmful habits and addictions. May those who are hooked on drugs and addictions too strong to control be given healing help that they may recover and be free again. Keep us from condemning the addictions of others and overlooking our own ungoverned passions. Enable us to be examples of serenity and self-control to the praise of the name of Jesus Christ.

O God, before you the generations rise and pass away. You are the strength of those who labor; you are the rest of the blessed dead. We rejoice in the company of your saints. We remember all who have lived in faith, all who have peacefully died, and especially those dear to us who rest in you. Give us in time our portion with those who have trusted in you and have striven to do your holy will. To your name, with the church on earth and the church in heaven, we ascribe all honor and glory, now and forever. Amen

Third Sunday of Advent

First Lesson - The prophet brings glad tidings of relief and renewal. Isaiah 61:1-4, 8-11

Psalm 126 or **Luke** 1:46*b*-55

Second Lesson - Paul urges cautious optimism as Christians give thanks and pray while waiting for the second coming of Christ. 1 Thessalonians 5:16-24

Gospel - John the Baptist, though a lesser light, is a light widening the eyes of people to see the brighter light of the Christ. John 1:6-8, 19-28

CALL TO WORSHIP

Leader:The grace of our Lord Jesus Christ be with you all.
People:And also with you.
Leader:Tell of the greatness of the Lord.
People:We will rejoice in God our Savior.

INVOCATION

Saving God, with joy we come to worship you and proclaim by our presence and by our attention that we are grateful for your many mercies to us and to all. You are worthy to be praised for the majesty of your creation and the grace of our Lord Jesus Christ. How great you are! Amen

PRAYER OF CONFESSION

Infinite Parent, Incarnate Offspring, Inclusive Spirit, in Jesus Christ you have experienced our humanity. We admit that we are not yet holy in spirit, soul, and body. Our worship is not always wholehearted. Our hearts and minds are often arrogant, prejudiced, unchangeable. Our bodies are too prone to rule us, and bad habits jeopardize our health. Forgive our faults and fulfill your promise through the communion of the Holy Spirit that we may be faultless when our Lord Jesus comes, to the glory of your great name. Amen

Prayer of Assurance

God of sure mercies and unbroken promise, we live secure in the faith of the church that you have made a covenant of salvation with us in Jesus Christ and bound it by the presence of the Holy Spirit with us and in us. Amen

[OR]

Declaration of God's Forgiveness

Pastor: Hear the Good News! God's mercy is sure from generation to generation, and firm in the promise to our ancestors that God will not forget to show mercy to their children's children. Friends, believe the Good News!

People: In Jesus Christ, we are forgiven.

[OR]

Declaration of Pardon

Pastor: Friends, hear the Good News! God's mercy is sure from generation to generation and firm in the promise to our ancestors.

People: God will not forget to show mercy to their children's children.

Pastor: Friends, believe the Good News!

People: In Jesus Christ, we are forgiven.

[AND]

Exhortation

Be always joyful. Pray continually. Give thanks whatever happens, for this is what God in Christ wills for you.

PRAYER OF THE DAY

Outgoing God, gift us again with the Holy Spirit that we may make way for you to the humble with good news; to the captives with promise of release; to the bereaved with the comfort of beauty and new gladness; to the brokenhearted with tender, loving care; and to the oppressed with the promise of eventual justice. Lord God, make righteousness and praise blossom before all nations. Amen

PRAYER OF THANKSGIVING

Hallowed be your name, mighty God, hallowed be your name, merciful God. Hallowed be your name, active God, you side with the humble rather than the proud, with the poor rather than the rich, with the powerless rather than the powerful. You come into our world in Mary's child, Jesus of Nazareth, the Son nearest your heart, full of grace and truth. Thanks be given to you always, in Hebrew and Greek and English and in every language of the universe. Amen

PRAYER OF DEDICATION

God, who promised to come, has come, and has promised to come again, we are preparing ourselves for your return and offer our gifts and ourselves to make the way straight for Jesus Christ our Lord. Amen

18

PRAYER OF INTERCESSION
AND COMMEMORATION

Creator God, continue your activity in the creation, maintaining and sustaining the forces that operate our galaxy in your universe, which you made and called good. Redeemer God, who has entered our sphere of life in Jesus of Nazareth, complete your saving work in our world, repairing the ravages of human disobedience and conflict so that peace may be more than a cessation of war, bombings, assassinations, plots, and counterplots and a perfect humanity finally be regained.

God of the prophets, inspire our young men and our young women to dream dreams of genuine prosperity and progress and peace. When age and illness make us less productive, give us grace to make places for those capable of succeeding us and carrying on the best of what we have begun and adding to it new projects and services that will enrich our common life.

Timeless Father, Eternal Brother, Mothering Spirit: you have set the solitary in families and seek to teach us to love others as we love ourselves, honestly and graciously. May we be teachable in every generation from the oldest to the youngest, knowing how great your wisdom is and how fallible we can be. Grant us the spirit of forgiveness that, confessing our faults to one another, we may forgive and be forgiven; through Jesus Christ our Savior.

God of past and future, dying and rising Savior, eternal and contemporary Spirit, hear our prayers for the people of your world, in which you live but in which there are also powers of evil and of death. Overcome evil in and through us. Call the nations of the world to new experiments in cooperation so that all the gifts of the earth's people may be put to good use for the common good. Guide the leaders of both management and labor to new ways of achieving economic justice in the sharing of profit and in serving fairly the needs of consumers.

Give wisdom to all who seek to redefine the borderline between life and death, which the medical community has expanded in so many ways that it is difficult to know what prolongs dying and what prolongs genuine human life. Give wisdom to government leaders as to the responsibility of parents and the limits of government intervention in private decision-making by individuals and by parents for their minor children.

Bless and uphold all who live on the borderline between life and death and those who keep watch with them. May your love and grace be sufficient for all.

Give continuing wisdom and skill to all medical personnel who look for new ways of healing and helping us to live longer. Bless as well all who are involved in hospice care and others who are also dedicated to helping us through the final valley of the shadow of death. May your grace, mercy, and peace be with the dying and sustain in hope those who die a little with them.

God of the living, we give thanks for the rest and peace of those you have taken to yourself. May we hear your gracious invitation above all other voices when the hour of our death comes. These and all our prayers we offer to you through Jesus Christ our Lord. Amen

Fourth Sunday of Advent

First Lesson - David is promised God's unfailing love and a long, disciplined dynasty to follow him on the throne. 2 Samuel 7:1-11, 16

Luke 1:47-55 or **Psalm** 89:1-4, 19-26

Second Lesson - Paul's letter to the Romans is concluded with a dignified doxology. Romans 16:25-27

Gospel - The angel Gabriel announces to Mary that she is favored by God to be the mother of God's Son. Luke 1:26-38

CALL TO WORSHIP

Leader:The grace of our Lord Jesus Christ be with you all.

People:And also with you.

Leader: Happy are the people who have learned to give acclaim to God.

People:We walk in the light of the Lord's presence.

INVOCATION

God of light, in whom is no darkness, in our darkest days we come to you seeking enlightenment and the guidance of the Spirit as you speak to us through your Word, written and human in Jesus Christ, who has taught us to pray. Amen

*12/9/01
Sun. nite*

PRAYER OF CONFESSION

God to humanity descending, man to God ascended, God to all condescending, you send prophets to lead adulterous royalty to repentance and angels to innocent, common folk to direct them in your service. Forgive any unwillingness we have shown to do your will, any reticence to proclaim the good news of Jesus Christ, any doubt that your promised kingdom will fully come and will not fail. We have not been prepared to serve you at the risk of personal reputation or at hazard of private wealth. Have mercy on us, for the sake of Jesus Christ, who served your purpose without reservation. Amen

Declaration of Pardon

Pastor:Friends, hear the Good News! The Divine secret kept in silence for long ages has been disclosed through the proclamation of Jesus Christ.

People:The prophetic scriptures have made known to us and to all nations.

Pastor:Friends, believe the Good News!

People:In Jesus Christ, we are forgiven.

[AND]

Exhortation

Come in faith and obedience to God through Jesus Christ that the presence of the Holy Spirit may make your standing sure, to the glory of God.

PRAYER OF THE DAY

God of all life, grant to all of us who are called to parenthood the gift of your Holy Spirit to develop our self-control, that in begetting and conceiving, we may give birth to holy children, dedicated to you by their baptism and nurtured in your service through our family life, by Jesus Christ, Son of the Most High. Amen

PRAYER OF THANKSGIVING

We will sing the story of your love, O God, forever. We will proclaim your faithfulness to all generations. You declare your true love in covenants made with humble nations. You reassure the lowly person of your gracious favor. You call young and old alike to serve your purposes and complete your loving designs. We celebrate the motherhood of young Mary and old Elizabeth. We mark again with great joy the birth of the Son of God, the son of David, the son of Mary, Jesus of Nazareth, known as Joseph's son. We worship you, God the sender. We worship you, Jesus, the sent One, Son of the most high and son of the most humble. We worship you, Holy Spirit, God in touch with our humanity. Glory be to God in heaven and earth. Amen

PRAYER OF DEDICATION

The most majestic music is not an adequate gift of adoration to you and yet you hear the simplest song. The most precious gift is beneath your notice and yet you receive whatever is given out of the deepest poverty. Let our gifts and our lives be worthy of you as they can be only in the grace of our Lord Jesus Christ and the enabling Spirit. Amen

PRAYER OF INTERCESSION AND COMMEMORATION

God of all, everywhere, hear our prayers this morning for all who at this season, when we especially like to be with family and friends, are separated from them. Grant that visits and gifts to those who are in hospitals or nursing homes or prisons may be the means of making your love more real to them.

Bless those who are busy in emergency services: those whose own safety is in jeopardy as they seek survivors of disasters; those who bring food and emergency treatment to fire victims; those who are on call in ambulance, fire, and police services.

Bless families who are separated by divorce or difficulty that the spirit of the season may mellow differences and bring comfort and accommodation especially for the sake of children.

Heal the sick; comfort the dying and the bereaved. May the good news of your advent in the birth of the Christ Child renew the faith of the doubting who may feel unloved and abandoned by you as by others.

Grant guidance and correction to the leaders of the nations that there may be continued negotiations between governments and allies that may diminish threats of conflict and make real the song of peace on earth, good will to humanity.

God of all times and places, we praise you for all your servants who, having been faithful to you on earth, now live with you in heaven. Keep us in communion with them until we meet with all your children in the joy of your eternal kingdom, through Jesus Christ our Lord. Amen

Christmas Eve/Day
(First Proper A, B, C)

First Lesson - In the darkness the prophet welcomes the light of the great king in the line of David who will bring justice and peace. Isaiah 9:2-7

Psalm 96

Second Lesson - The grace of God that was made personal in Jesus Christ is expected again. Titus 2:11-14

Gospel - In Bethlehem, a shepherd's town, is born the Savior who is Mary's little Jesus, a descendant of the great king, David. Luke 2:1-14 (15-20)

CALL TO WORSHIP

Leader: The grace of our Lord Jesus Christ be with you all.
People:And also with you.
Leader: Silence, everyone, in the presence of God.
People:God has come out of the sanctuary of heaven.

INVOCATION

God of mystery, God of revelation, God of joyful sound, we worship you with the most profound devotion and with the simplest wonder at the foot of a manger bed, singing in the Spirit so that our joy may be received as true worship; in the name of Jesus Christ. Amen

PRAYER OF CONFESSION

God of all worlds, ours seems at times like an abandoned one. We share in its sin, its darkness, and its despair. We feel that you have left us alone to find our own way out of the mess we have made of things. We have forgotten that the world was created by you, revisited by you in Jesus Christ, and is

24

still yours, a dwelling place of your choice for your Spirit. Forgive the belief that you are nowhere, that forgets that you are now here, in the Spirit of Jesus Christ. Amen

Declaration of Pardon

Pastor:Friends, hear the Good News! The Lord has come, and is coming again.

People:May the peace of God keep guard over our hearts and our thoughts in Christ Jesus.

Pastor:Friends, believe the Good News!

People:In Jesus Christ, we are forgiven.

[AND]

Exhortation

The Lord is near. Have no anxiety, but in everything make your requests known to God in prayer and petition with thanksgiving.

PRAYER OF THE DAY

Child of Bethlehem, Man of Nazareth, Christ of God, with Mary we treasure the stories of your birth and ponder them. May the celebration of your birth, both in this place and in our social circles, bring glory and praise to your name. Amen

PRAYER OF THANKSGIVING

Shepherd of Israel, Lamb of God, Keeper of Christ's flock, with Bethlehem shepherds of old, we come to see what has happened and consider what has been made known to us. We rejoice in the birth of this child Jesus who embodies both the Good Shepherd and the Lamb of God that takes away the sin of the world. For his obedience to your saving purpose we are thankful. That you become involved in the sin and suffering of our world, we are astonished. That you continue to draw us together as your flock by the Spirit, we are comforted. Amen

PRAYER OF DEDICATION

Not often enough, O God, do we offer you the gift of our silence, in adoration, in attentiveness, in anticipation of your directions. Receive us in this solemn moment and in such times of silence as we find for you in the days to come. Amen

PRAYER OF INTERCESSION AND COMMEMORATION

Almighty and ever living God, by your apostle you taught us to pray not only for ourselves but for others and to give thanks for all of life.

Heavenly Parent of all fathers and mothers and families: guard the laughter of children and their playfulness. Bring them safely through injury and illness, so they may live the promises you give. Do not let us be so preoccupied with our work that we fail to hear their voices or pay attention to them and their special vision of truth; but keep us with them, ready to listen and to love, even as in Jesus Christ you have loved us, your grown-up, sometimes wayward children. First Creator: by your love we are given children through the miracle of birth. May we greet each new child with joy and surround them with faith so they may know who you are and want to be disciples of Jesus Christ. Remind us never to neglect our children either physically or spiritually but to show them the loving acceptance that was the model given us by Joseph and Mary and by Jesus himself.

Inspire your whole church with the spirit of power, unity, and peace. Grant that all who trust you may receive your Word, and live together in love.

Lead all nations in the way of justice and goodwill. Direct those who govern, that they may rule fairly, maintain order, uphold those in need, and defend oppressed people—that this world may claim your rule and know true peace.

Give grace to all who proclaim the gospel through Word and Sacrament and deeds of mercy, that by their teaching and example they may bring others into your communion.

Comfort and relieve, O God, all who are in trouble, sorrow, poverty, sickness, grief, or any other need, especially those known to us whom we name before you in silence. Heal them in body, mind, or circumstance, working in them, by your grace, wonders beyond all they may dream or hope.

Eternal God, we remember before you those who have lived with us who have directed our steps in the way, opened our eyes to the truth , inspired our hearts by their witness, and strengthened our wills by their devotion. We rejoice in their lives dedicated to your service. We honor them in their death, and pray that we may be united with them in the glory of Christ's resurrection. Amen

First Sunday after Christmas Day

First Lesson - The prophet speaks of a divine presence more immediate than messenger or angel. Isaiah 63:7-9

Psalm 148

Second Lesson - The writer to the Hebrews explains the reason for the humanity of our Savior, Jesus Christ. Hebrews 2:10-18

Gospel - Matthew closely links the childhood survival of Jesus with Old Testament prophecies. Matthew 2:13-23

CALL TO WORSHIP

Leader: The grace of our Lord Jesus Christ be with you all.
People:And also with you.
Leader: With the whole congregation we will praise the
    great deed of God.

People: With the whole congregation we will praise God, who has won a name by marvelous deeds in Jesus Christ.

INVOCATION

Though you hear our unspoken prayers and the quietest whisper, O God, you rejoice also to hear the common voice we speak together in your praise and honor. We come to you in the confidence of children to their own parent because you have come to us in Jesus Christ our brother. Amen

PRAYER OF CONFESSION

God for all nations, we live still in a world where fathers and mothers and children must seek refuge from violence and bloodshed. We have learned little of the ways of peace, depending on the power of armaments to maintain governments and not sparing even children in the massacres of war. Forgive us if we have been advocates of war or indifferent to the needs of refugees. We need to learn more just ways of settling claims to govern and more equitable distribution of the good things you have created for us all to enjoy. Free us all to serve each other in Christlike tenderness, for your Name's sake. Amen

Prayer of Assurance

Holy God, though the perfection of Jesus Christ has power to judge our sinfulness you have chosen to accept his advocacy and priesthood on our behalf. We rely on him in confidence that you accept us graciously because of his intercession. We pray in the name of Jesus Christ. Amen

[OR]

Declaration of God's Forgiveness

Pastor: Hear the Good News! Jesus Christ has become like us in every way, so that he might be merciful and faithful as our high priest before God, expiating our sins. Friends, believe, the Good News.

People: In Jesus Christ, we are forgiven.

[OR]

Declaration of Pardon

Pastor:Friends, hear the Good News! Jesus Christ has become like us in every way, so that he might serve as our high priest before God, expiating our sins.

People:Jesus Christ has become our merciful and faithful high priest before God, sacrificing himself for our sins.

Pastor:Friends, believe the Good News!

People:In Jesus Christ, we are forgiven.

[AND]

Exhortation

Meet whatever tests face you now, knowing that Jesus is able to help us, having passed through the test of suffering.

PRAYER OF THE DAY

Whether in withdrawal or return, Great Overseer, help us to fulfill your purposes for us as individual and as families, acknowledging our need for each other and always seeking what is best for all of us. Give us patience to retreat and wait for the right time and courage to advance and confront when that is in line with your plans for us and for others; through your carpenter/Son, Jesus of Nazareth. Amen

PRAYER OF THANKSGIVING

God above time, God in our history, God in our present, we are thankful that you govern the times and seasons. Our times are in your hands, and we are grateful for times of joy as well as sorrow, for dancing as well as mourning, for the time of Christ's birth as well as his death. Our own families know these cycles of change as generations rise and pass away. We rejoice in the babies, the children and grandchildren among us, and in the long life which allows many of us to see them grow up. Hear our praise in voices young and old, high and low, weak and strong, until our time of silence comes. Amen

PRAYER OF DEDICATION

High God, you have not merely sent an angel envoy to us, but have come yourself to deliver us through Jesus Christ. We stand before you to offer ourselves, and not merely our offering, to serve you and others as one people, your people. Amen

PRAYER OF INTERCESSION AND COMMEMORATION

Eternal God, you have made your church like a burning bush that flames but is not consumed. As from the burning bush you called Moses to be your servant, so from the church aflame with the Holy Spirit, you call unbelievers to faith, doubters to confidence, and the wayward to walk in the way of Christ, who is the truth and the life.

Bless the church in all its mission in this country and in the most distant places in the world. May the name of Jesus be honored everywhere the good news is spread.

Universal God, you gave this good land to our ancestors as a heritage to be treasured by good stewards for generations yet unborn. Forgive any failures in maintaining this heritage and grant wisdom to restore what may have been laid waste.

Bless us with honorable industry, honest business, sound learning, and good manners. Save us from mischief, violence and disorder, from arrogance and every kind of exploitation. Defend our liberties and preserve our unity in diversity. Make our government leaders strong symbols of wise counsel and action that exceeds the limits of party considerations.

Heavenly Parent to the baby Jesus and all our children, show us how to care for all babies, especially the children of the poor, the disabled, and mentally ill. Save the children of parents who are alcoholics or addicted to other drugs and any who are sexually abused.

We pray for all who suffer pain from accident or illness, all who are chronically ill or disabled and those who are sick temporarily. Send them relief in body and spirit through medical staff and spiritual counselors.

Comfort those who have celebrated Christmas with the sadness of missing one who was with them until death intervened in the year that is passed.

We give you thanks for the prepared places you have made for those whose earthly struggle and service is completed. Bring us at last to the same place of peace and rest where we will be safe from sin and sorrow and be perfected from strength to strength and glory to glory through Jesus Christ our Savior, to whom, with you and the Holy Spirit, be all dominion and power, now and forever. Amen

Second Sunday after Christmas Day

First Lesson - There is reason for joy in the regathering of the people of God after their dispersal. Jeremiah 31:7-14

[OR]

Wisdom has a place of honor in the divine purpose. Sirach 24:1-12

Psalm 147:12-20 or **Wisdom of Solomon** 10:15-21

Second Lesson - God's earthly family is adopted through Jesus Christ to enlarge the heavenly family. Ephesians 1:3-14

Gospel - We are a new humanity through Jesus Christ and our rebirth through receiving him. John 1:(1-9) 10-18

CALL TO WORSHIP

Leader: The grace of our Lord Jesus Christ be with you all.

People: And also with you.

Leader: Sing out your praises and say,

People: God has saved his people.

Leader: See how the Savior brings them from the end of the earth,

People: the blind and lame among them,

Leader: women with child

People: and women in labor, a great company.

Leader: Young men and old shall rejoice,

People: then shall the girl show her joy in the dance.

Leader: God turns their mourning into gladness,

People: and gives them joy to outdo their sorrow.

INVOCATION

God of our hopes, Christ of our faith, Spirit in our hearts, we come to worship you with joy and gladness. Your goodness knows no limits of generation or gender, of condition or citizenship. You are kind to all, and we worship you in all sincerity; through Jesus Christ our Lord. Amen

PRAYER OF CONFESSION

All-glorious God, paternal, fraternal, maternal, we have faith in Jesus Christ, and love towards your people, yet we are not without blemish in your sight, not full of love, wisdom, and other spiritual blessings you still have available for us. Our love is not as inclusive as yours, and there is much we need to learn. Give us clearer vision of all that we are meant to be, so that by becoming fulfilled, we may increase the glory that is properly revealed in Jesus Christ, your beloved. Amen

Declaration of Pardon

Pastor:Friends, hear the Good News! The liberator has
come to free us from all proud pretenses.

**People:The Christ has come in Jesus of Nazareth to show
us the undeserved favor of God.**

Pastor:Friends, believe the Good News!

People:In Jesus Christ, we are forgiven.

[AND]

Exhortation

Accept the limitations of your own knowledge. Have reverence for the wisdom of the Creator. Be thankful for his love
in Christ and for a humble place in his house.

PRAYER OF THE DAY

Available God, whatever our age, whether married or single,
make us sensitive to what you are doing and about to do, that
we may not miss the excitement of being a part of the living
history that you are writing, through Jesus Christ. Amen

PRAYER OF THANKSGIVING

We give thanks, God of Job and Jeremiah, David's Lord,
Anna's Christ, Luke's Savior, that we have found your house
in many places. We have found places of prayer with the
swallows and the sparrows. We have sung your praise in a
quiet circle under the stars. We have enjoyed the choir of
many voices and the joyous sounds of musical instruments
and found inspiration and refreshment. Along our pilgrim
way you provide the cup that sustains both soul and body.
We are happy when we trust in you. Amen

PRAYER OF DEDICATION

God of all places, many of us return to this place again and
again, expecting spiritual refreshment and growth in grace.

Bless all that we do to make this a place of renewal for all who will come to Jesus Christ. Amen

PRAYER OF INTERCESSION
AND COMMEMORATION

To Jeremiah's prayer, "Save, O LORD, your people, the remnant of Israel," we add the prayer of Paul that the full number of the Gentiles come in and all Israel be saved. As Jeremiah saw the regathering of dispersed peoples from exile, so may we see everywhere those who are as sheep without a shepherd gathered into the fold of Jesus Christ.

Give both the church and our communities a heart to help the blind and the lame, those with child and those in labor, those who are slow to learn and those who are victims of an addiction. In our neighborhoods give us such a sense of community that the young may rejoice in the dance, and the young and the old be merry. Turn sorrow into joy by our mutual compassion and comfort.

May we share what we have with the poor, whether through public or private auspices, paying our just taxes and giving to such philanthropies as serve the special needs of persons with particular ailments and disabilities.

We pray for all who are sick and suffering in our homes and hospitals and for all who nurse them; for all who are alone and afraid; for those who are near to death and those who wait beside them; for those who are bereaved and needing to get on with life. Heal, comfort and sustain by your ever present Spirit.

God above, you have provided in Jesus Christ a highway to the eternal city. We rejoice in the safe journey of those who traveled with us on the Holy Way and, cleansed of their sins, have reached their heavenly destination. Keep us ever in this narrow way that leads to eternal life, through Jesus Christ, the Way, the Truth and the Life, who has already been received into glory and from whom (and from you) is sent the Holy Spirit as our companion on the way. Amen

Epiphany

First Sunday after the Epiphany (Baptism of Our Lord)

First Lesson - The prophet envisions the gentle strength of the Messiah. Isaiah 42:1-9

Psalm 29:1-11

Second Lesson - Luke records a brief of the introduction by Peter of Jesus the Messiah. Acts 10:34-43

Gospel - Jesus is baptized as if he were a sinner like us and is consecrated to be God's special Son. Matthew 3:13-17

CALL TO WORSHIP

Leader: The grace of our Lord Jesus Christ be with you all.

People: And also with you.

Leader: Ascribe to the Eternal the glory due to God's name.

People: We bow down to the Holy One in the splendor of holiness.

INVOCATION

To no idols, but to you, O God, we bow in worship, for you only are worthy of our adoration and thanksgiving for you give us life and hope. In our baptism you have also received us as brothers and sisters of Jesus Christ and blessed us with the Spirit who inspires these prayers through the same Lord Jesus. Amen

PRAYER OF CONFESSION

God of life and light and love, we confess that our own lives are too dear to us. By comparison we do not want for others as much as we want for ourselves. We want justice and power for our party or nation but not for all parties and nations. We have some concern for our own enlightenment but not for

36

the enlightenment of all people everywhere. Sometimes we need to have patience with ourselves: more often, patience with others. Forgive the narrowness of our vision and of our commitment to others and to you, Creator of Life, Light of our eyes, Universal Spirit of Justice. Amen

Declaration of Pardon

Pastor: Friends, hear the Good News of peace through Jesus Christ, who is Lord of all.

People: It is to him that all the prophets testify, declaring that everyone who trusts in him receives forgiveness of sins through his name.

Pastor: Friends, believe the Good News!

People: In Jesus Christ, we are forgiven.

[AND]

Exhortation

God has commanded the church to proclaim Jesus Christ to the people and to affirm that he is the one who has been designated by God as judge of the living and the dead.

PRAYER OF THE DAY

Condescending God, we also would conform to all that you require, both being baptized and baptizing in the name of God—Father, Son, and Holy Spirit. Grant us the assurance that we are your children, blessed and beloved, that we may obey you with joy. Amen

PRAYER OF THANKSGIVING

God of everywhere and anywhere, we thank you for Jesus of Nazareth and for all to whom he relates us, not only the apostles and Cornelius the Centurion in past centuries, but also the God-fearing of every nation in our own time. We celebrate the good news of Jesus, that he went about doing good and healing all who were sick in mind, body or spirit.

We remember with devotion his death on the cross for us and how, rising from the dead, he was witnessed by the apostles and women of faith, chosen in advance. We ascribe to you creativity, caring and covenanting. Give us life, granting us healing and forgiveness, gathering us into the church of Jesus Christ. Amen

PRAYER OF DEDICATION

God of glory, we respond to all you have spoken, in the wonders of nature, in words of the Scriptures, in the Word made human to dwell among us. We glorify you in the presentation of flowers and funds, words and music, and by our presence in this sanctuary, in the name of Jesus Christ. Amen

PRAYER OF INTERCESSION
AND COMMEMORATION

Mighty and everlasting God, when the earth was without form and void, you sent forth your Spirit to bring order out of chaos and light into darkness. In the fullness of time you sent your Son, Jesus Christ, to be the light of the world. Now again send out your Spirit like a dove to bring your olive branch of peace and reconciliation to a sinful and rebellious world. May the truth of Christ dawn brightly over the darkest places on our planet, that those who stumble in ignorance may walk upright as children of light.

Keep your church as the salt of the earth with its saltiness intact to preserve the best in our social life. May your faithful people be like yeast to leaven the whole loaf of our political life, that righteousness may be raised to higher levels and virtue pervade more of our public affairs.

As the Magi came seeking the King of the Jews, so may King David's greater Son continue to commission able evangelists and teachers and healers to the distant places of the earth to bring peace, good will to all nations.

Save our nation from the hidden power and open shame of gross national sins. Deliver us from unbridled greed and the exploitation of the poor. Emancipate us from the slavery of covetousness, which is idolatry. Liberate those addicted to alcohol and other drugs. Free those who are co-dependents of the addicted and whose own lives are also unmanageable. Overwhelm powers of godlessness and crime with the sharp truth of your word and the strong witness of your people.

Compassionate Parent in heaven, accompany with your presence those living through days of pain and anguish, weeks of sickness and weakness, months of grief and sorrow. Keep from despair those near to dying. May your peace possess them and give them final victory in Christ, who makes us more than conquerors.

As we believe in you, O God, we are not troubled, for we believe also in Christ. We rejoice in his revelation that in his Father's house there are many dwelling places. We are content to believe that he has prepared a place for our departed loved ones, and will come again to take us also to be where he is. May we live gladly in that faith and give praise to your hallowed names, Father, Son, and Holy Spirit. Amen

Second Sunday after the Epiphany

First Lesson - The servant of the Eternal is a light to the nations. Isaiah 49:1-7

Psalm 40:1-11

Second Lesson - Through Jesus Christ we know God's grace, receive all spiritual gifts, and are sustained to the end, when we will be found guiltless. 1 Corinthians 1:1-9

Gospel - John the Baptist titles Jesus the Lamb of God and heaven declares Jesus to be the Son of God who will baptize with the Holy Spirit. John 1:29-42

CALL TO WORSHIP

Leader: The grace of our Lord Jesus Christ be with you all.

People: And also with you.

Leader: Do not keep the goodness of God hidden in your heart.

People: We will proclaim God's faithfulness and saving power.

INVOCATION

As we are gathered in your presence, O God, we proclaim your faithfulness and saving power. Like the first twelve we have followed Jesus as our teacher and believe that he is your anointed servant. Through him we have received the Spirit without whom we could not pray as we ought. Accept our spiritual worship through Jesus Christ our Lord. Amen

PRAYER OF CONFESSION

Supremely powerful Person, you have shown us love as well as awesome strength. In Jesus of Nazareth you have come among us as one who serves. We confess that we often prefer to be served than to serve, to be masters rather than servants. Forgive our disposition to shirk your service when we may risk suffering in the hands of the cruel and uncaring. To be sent as lambs among wolves does not appeal to us, as it did not appeal to Jesus, who nevertheless was your Lamb to take away the sins of the world, including ours. Amen

Prayer of Assurance

Holy God, with John the Baptist, we have received Jesus as Christ, your spotless Lamb to take away the sin of the world. Having been assured of the forgiveness of our sins, we seek the Spirit's blessing in full measure that we may live in a way pleasing to you; through Jesus Christ our Lord. Amen

[OR]

Declaration of God's Forgiveness

Pastor: Hear the Good News. You are claimed as Christ's own along with everyone who invokes the name of our Lord Jesus Christ. Friends, believe the Good News.

People: In Jesus Christ, we are forgiven.

[OR]

Declaration of Pardon

Pastor: Friends, hear the Good News! You are claimed as Christ's own along with everyone who invokes the name of our Lord Jesus Christ.

People: Yes, We are claimed as Christ's own along with everyone who invokes the name of our Lord Jesus Christ.

Pastor: Friends, believe the Good News!

People: In Jesus Christ, we are forgiven.

[AND]

Exhortation

Go in God's strength to call back those who have turned away from God and the people of God. Be a light to all who live in the shadows.

PRAYER OF THE DAY

Baptize us with the Holy Spirit, divine Baptizer, that the Spirit of peace may abide with us, drawing us together despite the differences and distances between us. Gather us into unity in your church, to the glory of your name and the name of Jesus, who also accepted baptism for our sake. Amen

PRAYER OF THANKSGIVING

You have done many wonderful things for us, forceful God. You have freed us from traps and situations that frightened us. You have sent us on our way again with new plans for our future. We share with others the good news that you save all who put their trust in you. We praise you before others and seek to warn those who might fall into temptations that have threatened our lives. Your love and loyalty will always uphold us, faithful Sovereign, brave Champion, Emissary of peace. Amen

PRAYER OF DEDICATION

Founder of the church, when we are unsure of accomplishing anything as your people, you promise to renew our light, that our witness may be seen by many. Receive our moneys and all our talents of hand and heart and voice, to spread the good news of your grace and peace. Amen

PRAYER OF INTERCESSION
AND COMMEMORATION

Most Gracious God, you send rain and snow to water the earth and bless with beauty growing things in their season. Send also showers of blessing upon your church everywhere in the world. Keep us in faithful and humble proclamation of the faith and deliver us from crying faults and unhappy dissension that brings reproach to the name of Christ. Give qualms of conscience to those neglecting to meet together, as is the habit of some. Gather your people to encourage one another in the faith, and all the more as we see the Day approaching. Revive our congregation and the whole church that nothing may be left undone that we ought to do.

We pray for evangelists and missionaries that your Spirit may be upon them anointing them to preach good tidings to the poor, bind up the broken hearted, giving sight to the blind in spirit, and freedom to those enslaved by sin. May your kingdom come, and your will be done on earth as it is in heaven.

Remember those who toil while others rest: nurses who wake while patients rest, police forces who watch to keep the peace, firefighters who face hazard day and night, drivers and engineers and pilots who travel night and day to maintain delivery of mail and other necessary materials for our use. Keep us grateful for all those who work with us, and for teaching us all a reasonable sharing of work and responsibility in true community.

We pray for all who are passing through trials of mind or body or spirit testing. Save them from doubt with renewed faith and hope and inner peace. Be pleased to heal the sick, relieve those who suffer, and comfort the dying and the bereaved. Sustain those who are ridiculed for their faith by unbelievers and blasphemers. May they remember Jesus who endured such hostility against himself from sinners, so that they may not grow weary or lose heart. With them we look to Jesus the pioneer and perfecter of our faith, who for the sake of the joy that was set before him endured the cross, disregarding its shame, and has taken his seat at the right hand of your throne, O God.

Eternal God, you are served not only by your perfect Son, but worshiped by multitudes who have followed him to your exalted presence. Since we are surrounded by so great a cloud of witnesses, may we also lay aside every weight and the sin that clings so closely, and run with perseverance the race that is set before us to win at last the crown of ever-lasting life. At your throne we will also worship you, to whom, with the Son and the Holy Spirit, be ascribed all glory and love. Amen

Third Sunday after the Epiphany

First Lesson - The people who walked in darkness have seen a great light. Isaiah 9:1-4

Psalm 27:1, 4-9

Second Lesson - Allegiance to church leaders other than the Crucified and Risen One disjoints the body of Christ. 1 Corinthians 1:10-18

Gospel - Jesus begins his public ministry in enlightening preaching and calling disciples. Matthew 4:12-23

CALL TO WORSHIP

Leader: The grace of our Lord Jesus Christ be with you all.

People: And also with you.

Leader: Be constant in God's house all the days of your life.

People: Gaze upon the beauty of the Eternal One and seek the Eternal in God's temple.

INVOCATION

We have sought your face, O God, and found it revealed in the face of Jesus Christ. In the communion of the Holy Spirit, let us know you more intimately in our worship not only for our joy but for our certainty in sharing our faith with others; through Jesus Christ our Lord. Amen

PRAYER OF CONFESSION

Lord Jesus Christ, we confess that we have dishonored your name by our quarrels and dissensions. We have frequently bragged about our own denominations, at the expense of other denominations. We have guessed at the opinions and beliefs of others, without the patience to ask and to listen to them in order to understand. Too often we have stressed our

44

differences, without any appreciation of our common faith and baptism. Forgive such pride that projects our own "wisdom" and clouds the gospel of your cross; for your own Name's sake. Amen

Declaration of Pardon

Pastor: Friends, hear the Good News! Christ was crucified for us all.

People: We are not divided by our baptism by whomever we were baptized.

Pastor: Friends, believe the Good News!

People: In Jesus Christ, we are forgiven.

[AND]

Exhortation

Agree among yourselves and avoid divisions. Be firmly joined in unity of mind and thought. We are all followers of Jesus of Nazareth.

PRAYER OF THE DAY

1|05

Divine Educator, teach us in our churches. Proclaimer of the kingdom, preach to us in our chapels. Sacred Healer, cure us of our illnesses and infirmities. Light of eternity, dawn on all who dwell in the land of death's dark shadows. Amen

PRAYER OF THANKSGIVING

Light too dazzling for human eyes, Light in focus in human form, Light dispersed in human beings, you have increased our joy and given us great gladness. You have freed those who were oppressed and given new dignity to those who were demeaned. You have brought light and freedom where there was constraint and gloom. You have gathered children of light wherever the good news is preached, and sent them out as lightbearers to those living still in the land of death's dark shadow. We rejoice with all who have seen the light and known your healing and ingathering. Amen

PRAYER OF DEDICATION

You may be worshiped in tent or tabernacle, in temple or house, God- everywhere. We will acclaim you with sacrifices of praise and monetary offerings to maintain this house of prayer; to the glory of your name, Parent above all, ever loving Brother, familial Spirit. Amen

PRAYER OF INTERCESSION
AND COMMEMORATION

Having confessed our sins to one another and prayed for each other, that we may be healed, we seek, O God, the aid of your Holy Spirit, that our prayers for others in the name of Christ may be powerful and effective.

Hear our prayers for your church, holy and apostolic and universal. Add to the faith of your people knowledge and zeal and overflowing love from your Holy Spirit, that the name of Jesus may not be scandalized by rivalries nor marred by gross errors of doctrine or practice. Correct false teaching and heal divisions that weaken the witness of the church and its mission to the world that you love and for which you gave your Son on the cross.

You loved us, O God, when we were strangers from you, and you call us to love strangers, like our neighbors, as we love ourselves. Be with our friends and family members who live abroad in strange cultures, that they may be received hospitably, and may we be open as well to those who live near us but may not speak our language or share our culture.

Embrace the lonely and the weary with the comfort of your loving Spirit, and draw us all into close communion in your church.

Hear our prayers for all who are tempted and striving and sinning, for those who have shamefully denied you and have lost heart and hope. Gentle Shepherd, find the lost and return them to your fold.

Into your care we commit all who are dear to us. Sustain us in our relationships of interdependence, carrying our own burden but also sharing the burden of others when it is more than they can carry.

Hear our prayers for the sick, the aged, the frail, that they may know your healing strength and give thanks to you. Gracious God, we rejoice in the wisdom of Christ in his faithful people, who now have immortality and leave an everlasting remembrance to those who come after them. May we be like those who are wise, who shine like the brightness of the sky, and like those who have led many to righteousness, like the stars forever and ever. So may we bring glory to you, Fatherly, Brotherly, Motherly God. Amen

Fourth Sunday after the Epiphany

First Lesson - Micah comes to the heart of the matter in the conclusion of this reading. Micah 6:1-8

Psalm: 15:1-5

Second Lesson - Paul speaks of the paradoxical power of the gospel of the cross. 1 Corinthians 1:18-31

Gospel - Matthew gives us the values of Jesus in a series of blessings we call the Beatitudes. Matthew 5:1-12

CALL TO WORSHIP

Leader: The grace of our Lord Jesus Christ be with you all.

People: And also with you.

Leader: Depend upon God to grant your heart's desire.

People: We will commit our lives to Christ and trust the Spirit to do what is beyond our doing.

INVOCATION

God on high, we bow before you humbly but we cannot claim to always love kindness and do justice. Though we aspire to achieve this perfection, we can now offer only the advocacy of Jesus who has achieved such sinlessness before you. Continue the work of the Spirit in our transformation for your name's sake. Amen

PRAYER OF CONFESSION

Wise and mighty God, humble and gentle God, humbling and gentling Spirit, we confess that we do not always learn without pride or act with self-control. We forget the example of Jesus, who taught without arrogance and acted without domineering. Forgive us for undue regard for human standards of scholarship or rank or office, whether in others or ourselves. Excuse our proud boast of accomplishment that discounts what we owe to you and others and disregards the gap between our finiteness and your infinity. How foolish and weak we can be. Amen

Declaration of Pardon

Pastor: Friends, hear the Good News! God has made Christ our wisdom and righteousness.

People: In him we are consecrated and free.

Pastor: Friends, believe the Good News!

People: In Jesus Christ, we are forgiven.

[AND]

Exhortation

If you boast at all, let your boasting be about the Lord Jesus, who is God's wisdom and power.

PRAYER OF THE DAY

All-blessing God, in our search for happiness, save us from the expediency of the moment, the exploitation of the weak, and the exercise of selfish rights, that we may know the rewards that last, the mercy you offer the merciful, and the peace of your presence, through Jesus Christ our teacher. Amen

PRAYER OF THANKSGIVING

God of the gospel, Christ of the cross, Voice of the scriptures, we rejoice in the wisdom of the Eternal that you share with the humble. We accept with gratitude the salvation you offer to those who have faith in the doctrine of the cross. We celebrate with joy the overthrow of all that exalts itself against you. Let our boasting always be in what you do for us in suffering love and gentle wisdom and overflowing mercy. Amen

PRAYER OF DEDICATION

What shall we bring when we approach you, O God? How shall we bow down before the Most High? No offerings can atone for our sins. Christ has offered himself for us. Enable us to act justly, to love mercy, and to walk humbly before you, in the Spirit of Jesus Christ. Amen

PRAYER OF INTERCESSION
AND COMMEMORATION

God above, Christ ascended, Spirit descended, you have built us together spiritually into a dwelling place for yourself. In your love for the church draw us close together, that there may be no cracks in the pillars of your temple, and may gates of your holy place stand wide open to all who will come to you. May the Spirit and the church say, "Come." And let everyone who hears say, "Come." And let everyone who is thirsty come. Let anyone who wishes take the water of life as a gift. Grant peace in our time, O Lord. Bring an end to boastful rivalries, cruel threatenings, and crippling fears that lead to war and rumors of war. Bless every organization that seeks a negotiated end to rival claims of territories and political rights. Teach us how to beat swords into plowshares, armaments into reconstruction of what has been laid waste by war.

Guide the destinies of our own nation that we may live in security, with crime under control, the needy being helped, and the citizenry alert to maintain our liberty.

Great Physician, as you gave your disciples gifts of healing, so bless all who care for our sick and accident victims. Give wisdom to those who give care and to those who do research to find new cures for the diseases that plague us.

Eternal God, whatever is born of your Spirit conquers the world. And this is the victory that conquers the world, our faith. We give thanks for those who already enjoy the fruits of that victory in heaven with you and pray that we may continue to fight the good fight of faith and enter into your glory through the grace of our Lord and Savior Jesus Christ, your eternal love, and the communion and enablement of your Holy Spirit. Amen

Fifth Sunday after the Epiphany

First Lesson - Ritual fasting does not gain us the divine favor as brightly as benevolent social action. Isaiah 58:1-9*a* (9*b*-12)

Psalm 112: 1-9 (10)

Second Lesson - Paul specifies that the gospel of the cross is more persuasive than "wisdom" and oratory. 1 Corinthians 2:1-12 (13-16)

Gospel - The light of good deeds should point to the goodness of God. Matthew 5:13-20

CALL TO WORSHIP

Leader: The grace of our Lord Jesus Christ be with you all.

People: And also with you.

Leader: O praise the Lord! Happy is the person who fears the Eternal One.

People: We find great joy in God's commandments.

INVOCATION

Invisible God, you have revealed yourself to us in Jesus Christ, sharing your own Spirit in communion with our spirit. As we come to worship disclose yourself more fully as we hear your written word and pray in the Spirit of Jesus Christ. Amen

PRAYER OF CONFESSION

Creator - Restorer - Ruler: We are prone to point the finger at others and to pervert justice by exaggerated charges. We want the rich to feed the hungry, but not to share from our own provisions. We prefer charity in principle, but in practice evade our duty even to our own kin. Some of us live in half-empty houses while there are families crowded into rooms too small for them, if they have rooms at all. Forgive our failure to live up to the best we know and to let the oppressed go free even after you have freed us. Amen

Declaration of Pardon

Pastor: Friends, hear the Good News! Christ nailed to the cross attests the cost of God's love and forgiveness.

People: Our faith is not built on human wisdom, but on the power of God.

Pastor: Friends, believe the Good News!

People: In Jesus Christ, we are forgiven.

[AND]

Exhortation

You must shed light among your neighbors so that when they see the good you do, they may give praise to your heavenly Parent.

PRAYER OF THE DAY

Divine Householder, use us in our everyday work, that our faith may not be put back on the shelf or away in the closet. Make our faith evident not only in worship on Sunday but also in daily activities at home and elsewhere. Preserve the best of human culture and bring zest to daily life by the presence in the world of your church and its members, young and old, male and female, to the glory of your name. Amen

PRAYER OF THANKSGIVING

Maker of men and women, Parent of growing children, Teacher for all learners, we give thanks for all whose compassion is shown in more than overflowing emotions, who feed the hungry, find warm beds for weary travellers, carry water for thirsty workers, stop to help the stranded motorist. We praise the generosity of those who give freely to the poor, who give the shirts off their backs, who loan their cars and machines, who risk what they own on those whose credit is uncertain at best. Your Spirit moves them to act as well as speak. You will reward their obedience and ours, as we respond to your prompting. Praise to you, Source of all goodness and love. Amen

PRAYER OF DEDICATION

What you require of us, God of evenhandedness, is not self-denial for its own sake, but caring for the needy; not fasting for a rainy day, but to give food to the hungry. So we give, not that your house should be ornate, but that the light of the gospel may shine in worship and in public service, like the ministry of Jesus of Nazareth. Amen

PRAYER OF INTERCESSION AND COMMEMORATION

God of light and truth, you have sent your beloved Son to manifest your grace and truth. Make his church also to be the light of the world, a city built on a hill that cannot be hid. May our corporate worship in this place be like a lampstand that gives light to all in the house. In the same way, may our light shine before others in our daily life and vocation so that they may see our good works and give glory to you, our Father in heaven.

As iron sharpens iron, so may one person sharpen the wits of another. So bless the councils of the church and the state with the wisdom of our best and broadest minds, that both church and state may be saved from the narrow-minded and fearful. As you led your people of Israel in their journey into the unknown, so lead us into the future without fear and with less resistance to changes for the better.

Bless every form of education, that not only our children but we as adults may continue to learn not only about the new discoveries of science and exploration but also new relational skills in parenting and family life, conflict resolution in families and community life, and ways of peace among nations rather than war.

God of life and health, grant new vigor to the sick and weak, new hope to those who are discouraged and depressed, new directions to those who have chosen self-destructive ways of life. Bless every agency that seeks to promote such personal growth and healing.

Like our ancestors in the faith, O God, you have given us a desire for a better country, that is, a heavenly one. Therefore you are not ashamed to be called our God; indeed, you have prepared a city for us. We rejoice that you have already welcomed into that celestial city the many pilgrims who have preceded us in our journey. Sustain us also in our journey until we hear the trumpets sound for us on the other side of death; through Jesus Christ, our mortal but risen Lord, to whom, with you and the Holy Spirit, be ascribed thanksgiving and endless glory. Amen

Sixth Sunday after the Epiphany

First Lesson - The choice to obey or not to obey is the choice ultimately to live or to die. Deuteronomy 30:15-20

[OR]

The wise man seeks to define the line of responsibility between the human will and the will of God. Sirach 15:15-20

Psalm 119:1-8

Second Lesson - Cooperation, not divisiveness, is a sign of maturity. 1 Corinthians 3:1-9

Gospel - Jesus, the law, and the prophets expect respect not only in outward conformance to the tradition but in reconciliation of differences with others. Matthew 5:21-37

CALL TO WORSHIP

Leader: The grace of our Lord Jesus Christ be with you all.
People: And also with you.
Leader: Choose life. Love, obey, and hold fast to God.
People: We choose life. We will love, obey, and hold fast to God, for that is life for us and our descendants.

INVOCATION

Living God, we seek you with our whole heart though we are not entirely blameless and deserving of your gracious attention. Though we may be no longer in spiritual infancy, we have yet to grow to the maturity of Jesus Christ. Receive our prayers for Jesus' sake. Amen

PRAYER OF CONFESSION

God of all, we confess that we are all too human. We have our favorites among Christian leaders who sometimes receive the loyalty that only Christ deserves, and thereby make divisions among us. We are sometimes jealous of others and strive against each other instead of working as a team, as your coworkers. Forgive the immaturity, the unwillingness to rise above the natural plane, the parochial view that does not fully acknowledge one holy catholic church and settles for narrow denominationalism. We need to grow stronger, enabled by the Spirit to rise above pettiness, to broaden participation in your rule of earth and heaven, through Jesus Christ, our role model. Amen

Declaration of Pardon

Pastor: Friends, hear the Good News! Whether you are infants in Christ or more mature, you have the Spirit of God to stimulate your growth.

People: We have the Spirit of God to stimulate our growth.

Pastor: Friends, believe the Good News!

People: In Jesus Christ, we are forgiven.

[AND]

Exhortation

We are God's agents. Let us work as a team, and all of us will get our own pay for our own labor.

PRAYER OF THE DAY

Heavenly Sovereign, guide and goad us by both law and prophets to set as our highest priority making peace with our brothers and sisters, so that we may be properly prepared to offer you our worship and be ready for your just judgement. Amen

PRAYER OF THANKSGIVING

Heavenly Lawgiver, Sender of apostles, Inspirer of prophets, we give thanks for all whom you have sent to be our guides through the mazes of decisions that are before us in life. We rejoice in the diversity we find between Peter and Paul, between Elijah and Jesus. We celebrate the concerted service of Aquila and Priscilla, Barnabas and John Mark, and others who, like the twelve, found ways of serving you in a variety of combinations. We are grateful for individuals and couples and groups who have shared their faith with us and helped us to mature in our understanding of your will and supported us in our attempt to do your will. With great joy we remember them all and praise your name with them, an undivided company. Amen

PRAYER OF DEDICATION

As we offer our gifts, loving God, bring to our minds any unresolved grievance we may have with others, that we may continue the ministry of peacemaking to which we are called as followers of Jesus Christ. Amen

PRAYER OF INTERCESSION
AND COMMEMORATION

Founding God, Creative Son, Teaching Spirit, you have built your church on the apostolic confession that Jesus is the Christ. Preserve your church everywhere against the challenge of blatant materialism and self-centered morality. Teach us how to settle our differences among ourselves as well as how to confront the temptations in the world. Having forgiven our sins for the sake of Jesus Christ, give us a larger share of your forgiving Spirit.

God our governor, you have instituted government among us to provide for preserving law and order in our society. Bless all governing authorities, that they may be strong in confronting crime and examples themselves of good conduct. Teach us how to prevent crime and how to restore lawbreakers to lawkeepers, to do what is good, and receive your approval.

Bless all who work to restore to normalcy neighborhoods damaged by natural disasters or by acts of violence and war. Give patience to those who work with victims of crime as well as to those who seek to rehabilitate criminals. Repair our society, which has been eroded by the flood of illegal drugs. Save us also from the exploiters of sex and the glorification of violence.

Bless all schools and colleges, that our children may be wise in learning and loving in action. May they learn the appreciation of all human cultures and admiration for what is true and beautiful and good.

You, Lord, sustain us on our sickbed and in our illness heal all our infirmities. We are awed by the vulnerability you accepted for your eternal Son Jesus who has borne our infirmities and carried our diseases. Even more that he accepted death on the cross and was stricken, struck down, and afflicted for the sins of the world. He himself bore our sins in his body on the cross, so that, free from sins, we might live for righteousness; by his wounds we have been healed. Suffering Savior, be near to all who suffer that they may be comforted and healed.

Eternal God, as of old you went in front of your people Israel in a pillar of cloud by day, to lead them along the way, and in a pillar of fire by night, to give them light, so in all generations you go before your people. In the life and death, resurrection, and ascension of Jesus Christ, you have shown us the route we should take. We follow gratefully our ancestors who have followed the Christ in life, through death, and at last to glory. Ever keep us in the way of Christ that leads to life abundant and love unlimited.

To you Father, Son, and Holy Spirit be the glory and praise, now and forever. Amen

Seventh Sunday after the Epiphany

First Lesson - The holiness God requires is not piety alone but justice and compassion for one's neighbors. Leviticus 19:1-2, 9-18

Psalm 119:33-40

Second Lesson - Only what is built on the foundation of Christ will endure. 1 Corinthians 3:10-11, 16-23

Gospel - Jesus updates the commandments with startling changes to nonviolent behavior. Matthew 5:38-48

CALL TO WORSHIP

Leader: The grace of our Lord Jesus Christ be with you all.

People: And also with you.

Leader: Turn your hearts to God's decrees and not to selfish gain.

People: We will turn our eyes from looking at vanities; and will find life in the ways of God.

INVOCATION

Heavenly Parent, you are perfect as no earthly parent is. We come to worship you in order to emulate your perfection and to achieve in the Spirit a higher level of spirituality than we have known; through Jesus Christ our Lord. Amen

PRAYER OF CONFESSION

Generous God, we have not always been generous and caring for the poor and the alien. We have not always been straightforward in our dealing, and have defrauded our neighbors. If we have not stolen, we have not dealt honestly and have even sworn falsely by your holy name. We may profit from companies that ignore the needs of their employees to the advantage of the stockholders. We have not been careful for the needs of the deaf and the blind and other persons with disabilities. We have not protested the judgments that defer to the great or are partial to the poor. We have much to learn about your holy justice. Teach us by the words and example of your Son Jesus. Amen

Declaration of Pardon

Pastor: Friends, hear the Good News! Everything belongs to you: the world, life and death, the present and the future.

People: Everything belongs to us because we belong to Christ, and Christ to God.

Pastor: Friends, believe the Good News!

People: In Jesus Christ, we are forgiven.

[AND]

Exhortation

Share God's work in putting the land to rights and in caring for prisoners and others in distress.

PRAYER OF THE DAY

Perfect Parent, bring to perfection the love we have for others so that we love our enemies as well as our friends and become more truly "little Christs" to the honor of the name of Jesus Christ. Amen

PRAYER OF THANKSGIVING

We give thanks, O God, for your great wisdom and understanding of our humanity. For perfection you have created us, and with patience you work with us to fulfill the ideals of character that are most evident in Jesus Christ. We are thankful for the influence of the Holy Spirit, our family Spirit who draws us all into an always-loving relationship. We praise your name, loving Parent, caring Brother, tender Mother. Amen

PRAYER OF DEDICATION

God of love and power, we present our offerings and ourselves for your worship and service, setting our hearts on you and not on wealth to breed wealth. Use who we are and what we have for the eternal church of Jesus Christ. Amen

PRAYER OF INTERCESSION AND COMMEMORATION

Holy God, we approach your throne of grace with boldness, so that we may receive mercy and find grace to help in time of need, not only for ourselves but for others as well.

Hear our prayers for your church in this and every land, that all who confess their faith in Christ in whatever language and by whatever rites may do so in the Spirit who is the truth of Christ. Sustain us by your Holy Spirit so that we do not grow weary in doing what is right and so that we will reap at harvest time the fruits of our labors, if we do not give up.

As the church confronts opposition, remind us of him who endured such hostility against himself from sinners, so that we may not grow weary or lose heart.

We pray for all who hear your call and do not answer, who refuse your proffered grace, that they may reconsider your invitation and leave behind their sins and turn to you and the communion of your faithful people.

We pray for the poor and the homeless, for all who are left behind and forgotten; for the defeated, the timid, the broken-hearted, and all who are sick in body, mind, or spirit. Befriend, comfort and heal them for your name's sake.

Fatherly, Brotherly, Motherly God as you have received our beloved dead into the heavenly home prepared for them, keep us in communion with them by your guardian Spirit that we may come worthily to be received by your gracious love in Jesus Christ, to whom, with you and the Holy Spirit, be glory and majesty, dominion and power both now and forever. Amen

Transfiguration

First Lesson - God summons Moses to the top of Mount Sinai to receive the tables of the law. The "glory of the Lord" bursts through the clouds in view of the people. Exodus 24:12-18

Psalm 2:1-12 or **Psalm** 99:1-9

Second Lesson - Peter was an eyewitness of the transfiguration and personally heard the voice confirm Christ's divine sonship. 2 Peter 1:16-21

Gospel - Before the eyes of the disciples, the "ordinary man" Jesus shines with the dazzling brilliance of the light of God. Matthew 17:1-9

CALL TO WORSHIP

Leader: The grace of our Lord Jesus Christ be with you all.

People: And also with you.

Leader: You will do well to attend to the message of the prophets, because it is like a lamp shining in a murky place.

People: We will attend to the message of the prophets, until the day breaks and the morning star rises to illuminate our minds.

INVOCATION

Eternal God, we listen for your voice in the message of prophets and apostles, in the music of reverence, and the prayers of your people. Dawn again in our minds so that we may walk in your light today and through the days to come; through Jesus Christ our Lord. Amen

PRAYER OF CONFESSION

Majestic God, transfigured Christ, impelling Spirit, we confess that we do not frequent the place of deep silence where the voice of the sublime presence can be heard. Our minds dwell too much on lesser human figures than on your beloved Child, Jesus. Our reading of the prophets takes us too often to the familiar and avoids the difficult and the demanding. Forgive us if we have resisted the leading of the Spirit and missed further illumination that the Spirit can bring through Jesus Christ, your Favorite. Amen

Declaration of Pardon

Pastor: Friends, hear the Good News! The apostles share with us their experience of the coming of our Lord Jesus Christ

People: when he was vested with honor and glory from the sublime presence.

Pastor: Friends, believe the Good News!

People: In Jesus Christ, we are forgiven.

[AND]

Exhortation

Do not interpret any prophecy of scripture by yourself. The prophecies were written not by any human whim but by those impelled by the Holy Spirit to communicate to us the words of God.

PRAYER OF THE DAY

Keep us, good Lord, from preoccupation with our sacred history, and from the tendency to erect sanctuaries that would delay us from going on to other encounters with you in places of human need. Reveal your glory to us in quiet places of meditation and in noisy places of daily life. Amen

PRAYER OF THANKSGIVING

Transcendent God, all too soon our experiences of your sublime presence fade when we leave the awesome view of what you have created, whether in macrocosm or microcosm. We remember such experiences with thanksgiving. We rejoice in the awesomeness of your presence as communicated by the grandeur of architecture or the sweep of great music and art. We are humbly grateful for the sense of belonging when the Spirit draws us into genuine community with the Christ, and we too are favored and know your love. All thanks be given to you, O God. Amen

PRAYER OF DEDICATION

We worship you, magnificent God, with sincere reverence, knowing that no gift is worthy of you but that you graciously receive us and what we bring for the sake of Jesus Christ, your Son, our Lord. Amen

PRAYER OF INTERCESSION
AND COMMEMORATION

God of Moses and Elijah, Father of our Lord Jesus Christ, hear the prayers of your church who with the apostles are committed to worship your exalted Son Jesus of Nazareth.

Bless every house of prayer that has been built by your church. May they continue to be dedicated to the glory of your well beloved Son Jesus and to exalt no other person, living or dead. Save us from false Christs, who proclaim their own deity and infallibility, and from new religions that seek to replace our Savior Jesus Christ.

Bless this house of prayer, the pastor and readers, the elders and teachers, the visitors and helpers, the singers and musicians, all who serve to bring beauty to the sanctuary and reverence to your name by Sunday worship and daily service in your name. Bless all who maintain this place of prayer with their contributions.

We pray for our country and all its citizens. Bring to places of leadership people who exemplify integrity, and save us from leaders who would use high office to exploit others and serve themselves above all. Make our nation secure, incorruptible in dealing with national and international affairs.

We pray for homes and hearts clouded with sorrow, shadowed by abuse, darkened by doubt, distressed with disease and injury. Heal and enlighten body, mind, and spirit, that these homes may be filled with joy and praise.

Gracious God, we rejoice with all who have believed with the heart and confessed with the mouth and so have been saved. Having acknowledged Christ before others, they are now acknowledged by the Christ before your throne in heaven. Help us to make the good confession in the presence of many witnesses, that we too may take hold of the eternal life and behold your face in glory, through Jesus Christ to whom, with you and the Holy Spirit, be all worship and praise. Amen

Lent

First Sunday in Lent

First Lesson - The freedom to know good and evil is also the opportunity for temptation and disobedience by our first parents. Genesis 2:15-17; 3:1-7

Psalm 32

Second Lesson - As we share in the disobedience of the first Adam, we may also share in the self-sacrificing obedience of the second Adam, Jesus Christ. Romans 5:12-19

Gospel - Human temptations for Jesus and for us include sins of the flesh and the spirit, hunger, pride, and idolatry. Matthew 4:1-11

CALL TO WORSHIP

Leader: The grace of our Lord Jesus Christ be with you all.

People: And also with you.

Leader: Be glad in the Eternal One, rejoice, O righteous,

People: We will shout for joy, as we are made upright in heart.

INVOCATION

God of grace abounding, Christ for all humanity, Guiding Spirit, we come to worship you, turning away from whatever may tempt us to idolatry. May our contrition be genuine and our resolution to serve your purposes sincere; through Jesus Christ our Lord. Amen

PRAYER OF CONFESSION

Planter of gardens, Maker of humans, Shaper of minds, we confess that we would be like gods, knowing what is good and what is bad. We would like to make our own rules to live by and frequently do, but we cannot always escape the nagging sense of guilt, even when we have determined that our new rules are better than the old. Forgive us for living below the best we know, for projecting better behavior that would improve our human condition but being unwilling to change even some of our simpler habits of daily life. Replace our guilt with energy to change ourselves in the Spirit of Jesus Christ. Amen

Declaration of Pardon

Pastor: Friends, hear the Good News! Just as through human disobedience all became sinners,

People: so through Jesus Christ all shall become just.

Pastor: Friends, believe the Good News!

People: In Jesus Christ, we are forgiven.

[AND]

Exhortation

Receive the overflowing grace, the gift of justice, that you may live and reign through the one key person, Jesus Christ.

PRAYER OF THE DAY

Spirit of God, lead us safely through the temptation to live primarily for the satisfaction of bodily needs. Save us from presuming on your care at the other extreme and being careless with the life that is precious in the sight of the Creator. Preserve us from adulation of any human being, however attractive and powerful, that we may worship faithfully God in Jesus Christ. Amen

PRAYER OF THANKSGIVING

How generous you are, eternal and timely Giver! You give us a great abundance of life—human, animal, vegetable. You give us puzzles to solve with our minds. You give us beauty to admire, and inspire our artistry. You entertain us with cunning animals. You face us with moral dilemmas, and graciously forgive our failure to live by the best choice. You give us opportunity for adventuring in the world, to prepare us for the privilege of living with Christ in the world that is coming, where you are undisputed Ruler. With angels and all your creation, we will give homage to you, then and now. Amen

PRAYER OF DEDICATION

Nothing that we give you was made by us from nothing, but is our reshaping of what you have already created. Magnificent and merciful Creator, receive our gifts, rude and simple as they may be, but given from thankful hearts and hands. Amen

PRAYER OF INTERCESSION
AND COMMEMORATION

Hear, O God, the intercessions we offer on behalf of others. Gracious God, you have called us to be the church of Jesus Christ. Keep us one in faith and service, breaking bread together and telling the good news to the world, that all may believe you are love, turn to your ways, and live to give you glory; through Jesus Christ our Lord.

Remove the veil over the eyes of those who have not truly seen your grace and truth in Jesus Christ, that seeing they may believe and turning to him be forgiven their sins and converted to live anew in the companionship of the church.

Bless those whom you have called as evangelists, who leave home and kindred and travel and witness as apostles of Christ. Grant them health, strength, and safety, and graciously use them to lead the lost to Christ.

We pray for our country and our leaders, both civil and religious. Direct our counsels, rebuke our follies, purge out our social sins. Send peacemakers among us to settle our disputes locally, nationally, and internationally. Bless all who are feeding the hungry, clothing the naked, finding homes for the homeless. Grant us contentedness in a life of shared abundance and reverence for you and all creation.

Compassionate God, you console the downcast and send visitors to the lonely. Give healing and help to those who are sick and recovering from accident, surgery, or addiction. Grant rest to the weary, relief to the suffering, and pause for the overworked.

Faithful God, you have called us into the fellowship of your Son, Jesus Christ our Lord. As we walk in the light as he himself is in the light, we have communion with one another, those here with us and those already with you in heaven. Keep us in unbroken communion with your church on earth that we may at the last be reunited with those now in the church triumphant; through Jesus Christ our Lord, to whom, with you and the Holy Spirit, be glory and majesty, dominion and power. Amen

Second Sunday in Lent

First Lesson - Abraham's response to God's election is readiness to leave the past behind and begin the journey of faith. Genesis 12:1-4a

Psalm 121:1-8

Second Lesson - To be children of Abraham is to know the salvation possible through faith in God's grace, not perfect obedience. Romans 4:1-5, 13-17

Gospel - Rebirth by the Spirit is as mysterious as the source of the winds. John 3:1-17

CALL TO WORSHIP

Leader: The grace of our Lord Jesus Christ be with you all.
People: And also with you.

Leader: Come to the Eternal One, who will keep you from all evil and preserve your life.

People: God will keep our going out and our coming in from this time on and forevermore.

INVOCATION

We are drawn to worship you, God of Creation, by the mystery of your power to bring into existence what did not exist. We could be too awestruck to approach you except that the gospel of Jesus Christ assures us of your loving acceptance of our humble homage in faith and in penitence for our sins. Amen

PRAYER OF CONFESSION

World-loving Creator, Son-giving Parent, Life-giving Spirit, we confess our disbelief in the face of mysteries that we cannot explain. We fear and resist spiritual transformation as if you would change us beyond our own recognition. Though we cannot control the winds, we would attempt to program the Spirit. Forgive our doubts concerning your love and our restrictions on your purpose for us in Jesus Christ. Amen

Declaration of Pardon

Pastor: Friends, hear the Good News! Our faith in God, like Abraham and Sarah's, is counted as righteousness.

People: Our salvation is a matter of sheer grace.

Pastor: Friends, believe the Good News!

People: In Jesus Christ, we are forgiven.

[AND]

Exhortation

Do not be afraid of new experiences of God. Be enabled by them to go on as a more faithful disciple of Jesus Christ.

PRAYER OF THE DAY

Sovereign Spirit, so inspire us that the life within us may be holy as you are holy, and that, renewed from day to day, what should die within us is replaced by what should be everlasting. Amen

PRAYER OF THANKSGIVING

God of pilgrims, we rejoice in your presence with your people. You have led our fathers and mothers on journeys out of idolatry, slavery, and religious oppression to places of new insights, to time of further reformation, on missions of truth-sharing. We give thanks for the heritage of faith that is ours and for the riches of grace that are ours in Christ Jesus. As we share this heritage in our generation, bless all the families of the earth as you have blessed us, in the name of Jesus Christ. Amen

PRAYER OF DEDICATION

Not only in this sanctuary, but wherever we meet you in our experience, receive our offering of ourselves, God-above-all, that we may build altars there and serve others in your name. Amen

PRAYER OF INTERCESSION
AND COMMEMORATION

You are great, O God; for there is no one like you, and there is no God besides you, according to all that we have heard with our ears. Because of your promise, and according to your own heart, you have wrought our salvation in Jesus Christ and called us as a people to share the good news with all the nations of the world.

Bless and add to your church those who are coming to themselves and returning to the home of their parents in the faith. Pour your water of life on the thirsty land, and streams on the dry ground. Pour your Spirit upon your posterity, and your blessing on your offspring. Call your people to more constant prayer, more victorious faith, and such confidence in you that the coming of your rule may not be delayed by half-heartedness.

Bless this land we love despite its faults. Sustain our government leaders in administering just laws and governing us with wisdom and integrity. Save us from the self-seeking and factions that serve only their limited agenda rather than the greater good. Unite us in a godly harmony that works together with you to accomplish your eternal purposes for our global village.

Compassionate Christ, comfort your children who are faint from the struggle with the ailments and adversities of our mortal life. Speak tenderly to those who mourn.

Grant to all your people the wisdom from above, which is pure, peaceable, gentle, willing to yield, full of mercy and good fruits, without a trace of partiality or hypocrisy, so that your church may provide a welcome haven for all who need to find your love.

God of the ages, Source of all life, we bless you for all your true and faithful servants, whom you have gathered out of every nation and language through our Savior, Jesus Christ, who have his name and his Father's name written on their foreheads. Especially we give thanks for those dear to our remembrance who by faith fought the good fight and have won the victory. Give us grace to make sure our salvation by persevering faith and obedient service in your church on earth that we may in due time serve you with the nation of priests in heaven. To you, O God, we ascribe all glory and praise time without end. Amen

Third Sunday in Lent

First Lesson - Moses is counseled by God to assure the Israelites of his caring like the parenting eagle. Exodus 19:3-6

Psalm 95

Second Lesson - Paul outlines the growth that follows suffering when Christians share their pain with Jesus Christ. Romans 5:1-11

Gospel - John relates at length the encounter of Jesus with a Samaritan woman at Jacob's well. John 4:5-42

CALL TO WORSHIP

Leader: The grace of our Lord Jesus Christ be with you all.

People: And also with you.

Leader: By the power of God's Spirit, worship the Eternal who truly exists.

People: We will offer God the genuine worship that is desirable.

INVOCATION

Unfathomable Source of life, generous Giver of life, outflowing Spirit of God, we come to worship as those who have found a spring of water and return to satisfy their thirst again. Refresh our spirits by your Spirit; through Jesus Christ our Lord. Amen

PRAYER OF CONFESSION

God of all nations, forgive our biases and prejudices, our refusal to have dealings with those of other races and orientations of which we do not approve. Excuse our religious one-upmanship that seeks to exalt our own persuasion at the expense of others and that would rather debate non-essentials than find common ground and concerted action. We are convinced that we are right, and stubborn in resisting any evidence that we should change our minds. Soften such hardness of heart with the warm love of the Spirit; through Jesus Christ our Lord. Amen

Declaration of Pardon

Pastor: Friends, hear the Good News! We have been put right with God through faith.

People: We have peace with God through our Lord Jesus Christ.

Pastor: Friends, believe the Good News!

People: In Jesus Christ, we are forgiven.

Exhortation

Don't be stubborn. Listen today to what God says. Do not refuse to obey what God commands and miss the fulfillment of the promises made for us in Christ.

PRAYER OF THE DAY

Well-spring of eternal life, satisfy our thirst for life today and every day along life's journey through wilderness ways. Help us to find time, in these forty days and nights of Lent, and on all of our days, for spiritual refreshment and growth in grace, your grace, Lord, Jesus Christ. Amen

PRAYER OF THANKSGIVING

God our Maker and Remaker, we sing for joy to you, for you care for us and provide for us. You accept us despite our history of failures. By faith we experience your grace and the renewal of our relationship with you in Christ. We find it difficult to rejoice in our troubles, but we do rejoice in the endurance and hope which your approval brings. Above all, we give thanks for the gift of your Holy Spirit filling us with love for you and the hope of sharing your glory. Amen

PRAYER OF DEDICATION

For generations you have been worshipped in this place, God of our ancestors, Father of our Lord Jesus Christ. Whenever and wherever your children come to you, receive their offering of true worship through the universal Spirit. Amen

PRAYER OF INTERCESSION
AND COMMEMORATION

God our Savior, save us from sibling rivalry and pour out your love in our hearts through the Holy Spirit that has been given to us so that we may pray sincerely for all kinds of people everywhere.

We pray for your holy church in all its branches and for every member. Sustain the ministry of your people in the densely populated places as well as in the thinly populated expanses of the countryside. Rebuild the waste places, and make the wilderness like Eden, the desert like the garden of the LORD; may joy and gladness be found in your church, thanksgiving and the voice of song in congregations large and small. Cause righteousness and praise to spring up before all the nations.

We pray for our nation and for our state and community, that we may be united in our commitment to liberty and justice for all. Preserve truth, widen understanding, encourage dialogue, facilitate negotiation of differences, and prosper our farms and industries.

Lord Jesus, as you went in to stay with your disciples at Emmaus, come to our homes and tables. Like Zacchaeus may we change our lives so that our homes are worthy of your holy presence and are a place where strangers are welcomed in your name.

God of health and peace, give peace to troubled minds and anxious hearts. Comfort the bereaved and heal those who are sick. Receive into ultimate peace those who are dying.

Let all who seek you rejoice and be glad in you. Let those who love your salvation say evermore, "God is great!" With those who have already entered into the rest you have prepared for your people, we praise you. Bring us on our way rejoicing until, with them, we receive your final welcome to become good and faithful servants of Jesus Christ. To you be ascribed mercy, love, and power—Father, Son, and Holy Spirit, one God. Amen

Fourth Sunday in Lent

First Lesson - God prods Samuel to anoint a successor to Saul while the belligerent Saul is still on the scene. 1 Samuel 16:1-13

Psalm 23:1-6

Second Lesson - Paul calls the Ephesians to turn away from all dark deeds to live as children of light. Ephesians 5:8-14

Gospel - The blind man not only has his eyes healed but also is by stages convinced that Jesus is the Christ. John 9:1-41

CALL TO WORSHIP

Leader: The grace of our Lord Jesus Christ be with you all.

People: And also with you.

Leader: Christ is the light of the world. As Christians you are light and should leave darkness behind.

People: We will live like those who feel at home in daylight.

INVOCATION

God of light, in whom there is no darkness at all, we are not blinded by your glory though we are dazzled by it even as it is refracted in Jesus Christ your Son. Fill us with your light so that the darkness still within us will gradually disappear; in the Spirit of Jesus Christ. Amen

PRAYER OF CONFESSION

One true Judge, your know us better than we know ourselves. You know our hearts and our thoughts, our motives as well as our actions. We confess that we tend to judge others and ourselves too much by appearances, by physical graces, by traditional manners rather than spontaneous helpfulness, by announced intentions rather than actual behavior. We would dread your true judgment, except for the mercy and goodness you offer us in Jesus Christ. Amen

Prayer of Assurance

Healing God, we are no longer blind but can see you as the source of all beauty, truth, and love. We are no longer children of darkness but children of your light in Jesus Christ. Amen

[OR]

Declaration of God's Forgiveness

Hear the Good News! Though you once were all darkness, now as Christians you are light. Friends, believe the Good News! In Jesus Christ, we are forgiven.

[OR]

Declaration of Pardon

Pastor: Friends, hear the Good News! Though you once were all darkness, now as Christians you are light.

People: Though we once were darkness, now as Christians we are light.

Pastor: Friends, believe the Good News!

People: In Jesus Christ, we are forgiven.

[AND]

Exhortation

Live like those who are at home in the light, for where the light is, there all goodness springs up, all justice and truth.

PRAYER OF THE DAY

Light Source, Light of our eyes, Light of our souls, open our eyes that we may see clearly and honestly, making judgments as you make them, and, turning from all darkness, live in the light of truth and goodness and justice for all. Amen

PRAYER OF THANKSGIVING

Generous Provider, you pour out such great blessings that our cup runs over. Anointing Spirit, you touch us with the oil of gladness and make our faces shine with joy. Heaven-sent Healer, you do God's work with great simplicity, healing our sicknesses and restoring our souls. We give thanks to you and worship you with slowly-deepening appreciation. Glory be to you, Light-above-us, Light of the world, Light-within-us. Amen

PRAYER OF DEDICATION

Divine Sovereign, elector and reject of earthly rulers, only the Holy Spirit can hallow us to appear before you, and only the Spirit enables us to perform any service worthy of offering to you. Receive what we offer for the sake of great David's greater Son, even Jesus Christ. Amen

PRAYER OF INTERCESSION
AND COMMEMORATION

Heavenly Parent, hear our prayers for our brothers and sisters in Christ which we bring in the name of our Lord Jesus.

Let no sibling rivalry disturb our family unity in the church. Teach us how to work together not only in congregations but in denominations and councils of churches. May the Spirit of Christ unite us in the bond of peace.

Bless our nation and its leaders. Advance the influence of the church in its commitment to truth and grace, education and human development, homes for the homeless, food for the hungry, and medicine for the sick.

Bless the medical establishment, hospital administrators and health insurance programs, doctors, nurses and technicians, bedside care and medical research, that the ministry of healing may be continued with care for all who require it. Bless pastors, chaplains, and hospital visitors who also seek to encourage patients and bring healing of mind and spirit to the sick in your name.

Bless those known to us whose chronic illness, temporary sickness, or emotional distress are of special concern to us. Bring healing of body, mind, and spirit with medical attention and prayer and human caring.

Bless every ministry to the blind or seeing-impaired. May the spoken word as well as braille publications communicate your word to those whose spiritual sight may be as keen as ours.

Eternal God, we have this hope, a sure and steadfast anchor of the soul, a hope that enters the inner shrine behind the curtain, in the Holy of Holies in heaven. We rejoice for the great multitude and our own loved ones who have already entered there by the new and living way that Christ has opened for us through the curtain. Draw us at last into that final refuge and harbor from the storms of this life; through Jesus Christ your Son, who lives and reigns with you and the Holy Spirit, time without end. Amen

Fifth Sunday in Lent

First Lesson - The prophet is given a vision of hope for the restoration, the resurrection of Israel. Ezekiel 37:1-14

Psalm 130:1-8

Second Lesson - Paul writes of the spiritual resurrection from the death of sin that the Spirit can perform. Romans 8:6-11

Gospel - In the account of the resurrection of Lazarus, John records some of the most profound promises of our Lord Jesus Christ. John 11:1-45

CALL TO WORSHIP

Leader: The grace of our Lord Jesus Christ be with you all.

People: And also with you.

Leader: Open your heart to the Spirit of hope.

People: Like someone in the darkness we will look for the first light of dawn.

INVOCATION

God in whom we rely, Christ in whom we have faith, Spirit of all our hopes, we come to worship you and to affirm our confidence in your love. We love you because you first loved us. Hear our prayers in the name of Jesus Christ. Amen

PRAYER OF CONFESSION

God of our yesterdays, our todays, and our tomorrows, we are too prone to live for the moment, to let our health and our emotions and our passions rule our lives. You offer us the Spirit to bring these things into wholeness under your control, but we resist and often are overtaken by events and sink into despair. From the depths you would raise us, if we cry out to you, but at times it seems we prefer sullen silence. Forgive self-pity that closes you out. We pray in the name of Jesus Christ. Amen

Declaration of Pardon

Pastor: Friends, hear the Good News! In the Lord is love unfailing, and great is his power to set us free.

People: God alone sets us free from all our sins.

Pastor: Friends, believe the Good News!

People: In Jesus Christ, we are forgiven.

[AND]

Exhortation

Live on the level of the Spirit. Keep the spiritual outlook that
is life and peace.

PRAYER OF THE DAY

this evening

Loose us, living Lord, from ~~the fear of~~ death and its power, to
live freely the life of the Spirit, ~~in obedience to your com-~~
~~mand~~, so that, invigorated by the indwelling Spirit, we may *truly live*
and accomplish your purposes, to the glory of your name. Amen

PRAYER OF THANKSGIVING

Living God untouched by death; incarnate Son of God, Con-
queror of death; life-giving Spirit of God; we tax our minds
and our language to praise you, even to name you. No
thanksgiving we offer is adequate. Human life is a mystery:
your life even more so. Your love for us mortals, like the love
of Jesus for Lazarus defies description. We find unending joy
in the assurance of your love and the promise of eternal life
with you and with all whom we love. Amen

PRAYER OF DEDICATION

These offerings, good Lord, are life giving only as your Spirit
enables us as the church to do your work in the world. Bless
and use us in your service of others. Amen

PRAYER OF INTERCESSION
AND COMMEMORATION

Spirit of truth, you have taught us that we do not live to
ourselves, and we do not die to ourselves. So you urge us to
pray not only for ourselves but for others, that together,
whether we live or whether we die, we are the Lord's. Free

your church from any captivity to the limited truth of political parties and secular philosophy.

May the whole truth of Christ be our ideal for daily life. Trusting in the power of the living word in Christ, and speaking the truth in love, may we draw outsiders into the church with the gracious invitation of your gospel. So may your church grow in numbers and influence wider society.

Sustain public leaders who profess their loyalty to your church that their announced policies and actual practice may be consistent with their declared faith. Protect them from false accusation and the assassin's attack. Grant them patience amidst great provocation.

God of grace, in Jesus Christ you entered the sick room with healing and in the streets responded to the cries of the helpless. Continue his healing ministry in our hospitals and nursing homes and home nursing systems. As he also fed the hungry on occasion, bless all hunger programs that seek to bring aid to famine-stricken lands and self-help projects that seek to help people feed themselves and their neighbors.

Living Lord, fulfill your promise to be the resurrection and the life, that all who believe in you, even though they die, will live again. Take to yourself our dying family members and friends, from the suffering of this life to the joys of immortality. At the time you have appointed take us also to be with them and with you to the glory that is beyond our imagining. To God our Father, and Jesus our Brother and the Holy Spirit our Mother be ascribed all grace and glory. Amen

Sixth Sunday in Lent

First Lesson - Learning to listen patiently to God can develop wisdom in speech and confident patience under persecution. Isaiah 50:4-9*a*

†**Psalm** 118:1-2, 19-29 († = As Palm Sunday)
††**Psalm** 31:9-16 (†† = As Passion Sunday)

Second Lesson - If the elect offspring of God can accept humble servanthood and suffering, why not those of us who take the name Christian? Philippians 2:5-11

†**Gospel** - A humble king is welcomed as he comes riding a gentle donkey. Matthew 21:1-11
††**Gospel:** Jesus Christ, the ultimate Judge experiences human justice and injustice. Matthew 26:14–27:66 or Luke 27:11-54

†/††CALL TO WORSHIP

Leader: Open to me the gates of righteousness
People: that I may enter through them and give thanks to the Lord.
Leader: This is the gate of the Lord;
People: the righteous shall enter through it.

†/††INVOCATION

We thank you, Eternal God, that you have answered us and have become our salvation through the human pilgrimage of Jesus Christ—doing good, healing the sick, suffering unjustly, dying heroically, and rising victoriously. Vicariously and in reality help us to join you in your suffering in conflict with evil that we may worship you here and hereafter. Amen

†/††PRAYER OF CONFESSION

Court of last appeal, we are too ready to judge others and to defend ourselves. We are impatient that you should set things right and vindicate our "good name." We are more prone to insult others than to accept slight and insult with patience. Rather than turn the other cheek, we lash out with as much vehemence as we can gather. Rather than keep silence, we resort to name calling and other verbal abuse. Forgive our short tempers and abuse of others, for the sake of the forebearing Christ. Amen

†/††Declaration of Pardon

Pastor: Friends, hear the Good News! God raised Jesus to the heights and bestowed on him the Name above all names.

People: God's Child came in humility as a human to the lowliness of servanthood and the shame of a criminal's death for our salvation.

Pastor: Friends, believe the Good News!

People: In Jesus Christ, we are forgiven.

[AND]

†/††Exhortation

Let your bearing toward one another arise out of your life in Christ Jesus.

†PRAYER OF THE DAY

Sovereign Jesus, after the excitement of the parade has passed, grant us pause to meditate on the majesty of your gentleness and the truth of what you teach and what you are, for we would become more like you as bearers of the name Christian. Amen

††PRAYER OF THE DAY

Divine Parent, whenever we think life is unfair to us or that we are given more than our share of suffering, remind us of the patience of Jesus and his trust, despite feeling of abandonment, so that our faith will not fail and our trust in you gives evidence that we also are your children. Amen

†/††PRAYER OF THANKSGIVING

God of glory, God of grace, we rejoice with humble hearts as we celebrate the condescension of the One who was your equal but left such glory for a while, to become human, in the lowliness of servitude, the pain of suffering, and the indignity of death. We raise our voices in exultation that you exalt the Christ again in raising him to the heights and bestowing on him the supreme name in the whole universe, announcing that Jesus the anointed is Lord. All glory be given to you, in praise of your vulnerability and your victory, one God, great in grace and great in glory. Amen

†/††PRAYER OF DEDICATION

No offering that we bring can compare, O God, with the offering of your Son Jesus and the self-offering that he makes on the cross. Nevertheless, may that example move us beyond giving to the genuine offering of ourselves in obedient service at all costs, for Jesus' sake. Amen

†/††PRAYER OF INTERCESSION AND COMMEMORATION

Heavenly Parent, your special Son, Jesus, became like us, his brothers and sisters, in every respect so that he might be a merciful and faithful high priest in serving before you. Since you have received his sacrifice of atonement for our sins, receive also our ministry of intercession in the Spirit.

O Lord, save your people, and bless your heritage; be their shepherd, and carry them forever. Give your church the same compassion as our savior and shepherd, embracing little children, gentling mothers to be, feeding the hungry, anointing the wounded, cradling the weak and dying. Bring back to your fold those who have wandered away into wickedness or indifference or irreverence.

Bless our nation, leaders and people alike, that with a common reverence of your name and obedience to your law we may find new prosperity and peace. Save us from the worship of wealth and the dependence on brute force. Restrain our pride and rebuke our prejudices. Give us mutual respect and love as children of one heavenly Parent.

God of compassion, show your mercy to the parents of dying children. As one whose earthly Son was killed in the prime of life, you know the sorrows of a dying Son who was a man of sorrows and acquainted with grief. By your power you raised Jesus from death to give us hope in believing. To him you have received all who believe in him for everlasting life. When our time comes, receive us also for the sake of hime who loved us and gave himself for us, Jesus our dying Savior and Risen Lord, to whom, with you and the Holy Spirit, be all praise and thanksgiving time without end. Amen

*E*aster

Easter

First Lesson - Here is an early outline of Peter's sermon, the heart of the Gospel, which will be preached to the ends of the earth. Acts 10:34-43

[OR]

As Israel once found grace in the wilderness, an even greater grace and restoration awaits them, declares the prophet. Jeremiah 31:1-6

Psalm 118:1-2, 14-24

Second Lesson - Paul promises a spiritual resurrection for us as profound as the resurrection of Jesus from death. Colossians 3:1-4

Gospel - The dearest friends of Jesus discover the empty tomb, and Mary Magdalene actually meets the Risen Christ. John 20:1-18

[OR]

Two women who followed Jesus were the first witnesses of the resurrection on the first day of the week. Matthew 28:1-10

CALL TO WORSHIP

Leader: The grace of our Lord Jesus Christ be with you all.
People: And also with you.
Leader: This is the day on which our Lord has risen.
People: Christ has risen! We exult and rejoice.

INVOCATION

God of unending life, on this and every Sunday we celebrate the rising of your eternal Son from the night of human mortality to the glory of your never darkened day. Receive our celebration of joy in the Spirit of our living Lord Jesus Christ. Amen

88

PRAYER OF CONFESSION

God of heaven and earth, God of flesh and spirit, Spirit of God and of the church, the world is too much with us; late and soon, getting and spending, we lay waste our powers, as it is not so much the harmony with nature that we have lost but our accord with heaven. What we excuse as merely human, you have condemned as sinful. We squirm at the description of our faults by prophets and apostles, not prepared to abandon our old ways because we have not lifted our eyes beyond the present state of things to the realm above and to the eternity beyond death. Forgive our lack of vision and spiritual aspiration, for the sake of your Son, Jesus Christ. Amen

Declaration of Pardon

Pastor: Friends, hear the Good News! Jesus Christ is the one who has been designated by God as Judge of the living and the dead.

People: We trust in him and receive forgiveness of sins through his name.

Pastor: Friends, believe the Good News!

People: In Jesus Christ, we are forgiven.

[AND]

Exhortation

Aspire to the realm above, where Christ is, seated at the right hand of God, and let your thoughts dwell on that higher realm, not on this earthly life. Now your life lies hidden with Christ in God. When Christ, who is our life, is manifested, then you too will be manifest with him in glory.

PRAYER OF THE DAY

Living God, dying and rising Christ, life-giving Spirit, save us from our doubts and fears. Enrich our lives with a growing knowledge of the scriptures so that the unfolding story of our life and death may bring new understanding of your word in wisdom for living and sharing with others on our way. Amen

LITANY OF THANKSGIVING

Leader: It is good to give thanks to you, O God,
People: for your love endures forever.
Leader: We declare it with the House of Israel,
People: for your love endures forever.
Leader: We declare it with the church of the risen Christ,
People: for your love endures forever.
Leader:We declare it with seeking disciples,
People: for your love endures forever.
Leader: We declare it with the bereaved and dying,
People: for your love endures forever, in Jesus Christ, crucified and risen. Amen

PRAYER OF DEDICATION

Miracle working God: what others reject as useless, you accept and utilize. We give ourselves and our offerings, in the confidence that you will make valuable what might have been wasted; through Jesus Christ, who is alive and with you, and through the Spirit who is with us. Amen

PRAYER OF INTERCESSION
AND COMMEMORATION

You are good to all, O God, and your compassion is over all you have made. Hear our intercessions in the name of Jesus Christ who was with you when you created the world and whom you gave to the world because you loved us so much.

Renew the church by your life-giving Spirit, teaching us everything we need to know and reminding us of all that

Jesus said to his disciples. Enable the church by the same Spirit to do even greater works than his, because he returned to you. May your healing Spirit close the wounds that the body of Christ suffers until the present day, uniting our angry divisions to the glory of the name of Christ.

Abba, Father, Holy Parent, we hallow your name and pray that your kingdom will come and your Son the Prince of Peace be worshipped everywhere in the world as the victor over sin and death.

Bless our land and all lands with freedom to hear and believe the good news of Christ's death and resurrection, and free those who all their lives were held in slavery by the fear of death. Give to the younger generation a firm faith in the rule of righteousness and truth that supersedes the best of human governments and judges all nations.

As in the days of Jesus on earth, when some people came to him bringing a paralyzed man, carried by four of them, we carry to you by our prayers those who cannot come to this sanctuary to pray. By your living Spirit visit the beds of the sick, the weak, and the aged. Encourage and heal and give strength according to their day.

To those who are bereaved give comfort through the Easter story of resurrection to everlasting life. Keep us all in the way that leads to life so that at the last we may be reunited with those whom we have loved and lost awhile. And to you, God of life, Risen Lord, and Living Spirit, be ascribed all glory and praise time without end. Amen

Second Sunday of Easter

First Lesson - Peter calls Israel by his bold preaching to believe the apostolic witness of the resurrection of Jesus. Acts 2:14*a*, 22-32

Psalm 16

Second Lesson - Even those who were not first-person witnesses of the resurrection of Jesus can love the one unseen and have salvation through their faith. 1 Peter 1:3-9

Gospel - Thomas and all doubters are invited to believe in the Risen Christ. John 20:19-31

CALL TO WORSHIP

Leader: The grace of our Lord Jesus Christ be with you all.

People: And also with you.

Leader: Come to worship with exulting heart and rejoicing spirit.

People: Bless our God who has given us counsel.

INVOCATION

Eternal One, Risen Christ, life-giving Spirit, we come seeking your wisdom. We celebrate the resurrection of Jesus with great joy for what hope and understanding it has given us in facing death and what lies beyond. Receive our worship and renew our faith in the communion of the Holy Spirit. Amen

PRAYER OF CONFESSION

God of creation and resurrection; Savior by birth, death, and resurrection; Spirit of our rebirth into hope; we confess that we can take our hope for granted. The passing of Easter year after year is accepted as routine, and we forget that the first Easter is unique in human history. If we give short shrift to the significance of the resurrection of Jesus, forgive such indifference. The death of a loved one or the imminence of our own death will test our faith soon enough, and we need a strong faith to sustain us; in the living Lord. Amen

Declaration of Pardon

Pastor: Friends, hear the Good News! God has given us a new birth.

People: With great mercy God has given us a living hope, through the resurrection of Jesus Christ from the dead.

Pastor: Friends, believe the Good News!

People: In Jesus Christ, we are forgiven.

[AND]

Exhortation

Trust the Christ you cannot see and love him with joy beyond words for that faith brings at last the salvation of your soul.

PRAYER OF THE DAY

Loving God, in a doubting world, keep us alive in our faith that Jesus is our Messiah, your Son and our brother, that we may have life in his name. Amen

PRAYER OF THANKSGIVING

God of purpose, portents, and plans, no rebel power can defeat your final purposes, and we look for continuing signs that your objectives will be realized. In Jesus of Nazareth you fulfill ancient promises to David, not with earthly pomp and circumstance, but with heavenly power over death through resurrection. No ancient throne can bring us gladness, but the presence of the Living Christ through the Spirit brings us joy and hope of eternal life. We are filled with thanksgiving in the confidence that you do not abandon us in death but lead us on in the way of life. All glory be given to you, O God. Amen

PRAYER OF DEDICATION

Sovereign God, though you can accomplish your purposes despite the wicked and the evil use of money, we would rather be among your disciples, serving you knowingly with what we have and what we are, in obedient faith. Amen

PRAYER OF INTERCESSION
AND COMMEMORATION

Father of lights, with whom there is no variation or shadow due to change, every generous act of giving, with every perfect gift, is from you. As children of your light we pray for children of darkness in the name of Christ who caused the blind to see and the lame to walk. Like the prophet Isaiah may we give the invitation: "Come, let us walk in the light of the LORD!" And "if we walk in the light as he himself is in the light, we have fellowship with one another, and the blood of Jesus [your] Son cleanses us from all sin." We pray for your church in this and every land that it may be staunch and obedient to the truth of Christ.

We pray for our beloved country and our leaders. Cleanse our public life from corruption, from faction and hostility, and incline all citizens to purity, temperance, and faith in your Word. Deliver us from a haughty spirit and contempt for other races and nations, and help us to spread the light of freedom in the world.

As the centurion confessed to Jesus "Lord, I am not worthy to have you come under my roof," so we pray: "but only speak the word, and [our friends] will be healed." Cure disease. Bind up broken hearts. Mend broken bones. Calm frazzled nerves. Speak peace to the guilty and repentant. O Lord Jesus, save all who call upon you.

Compassionate God, to you our parents in the faith cried, and were saved; in you they trusted, and were not put to shame. As you have glorified your Son Jesus in resurrection and ascension, you have given them eyes to see his glory, which you have given him because you loved him before the foundation of the world. In like faith we have put our trust in you and are sure that you are able to guard until that glorious day what we have entrusted to you. With saints in glory everlasting, we praise your name, Father, Son, and Holy Spirit, One God, eternally. Amen

Third Sunday of Easter

First Lesson - Peter's sermon is a call to repentance and a promise of salvation to his hearers and their children and those still at a distance. Acts 2:14a, 36-41

Psalm 116:1-4, 12-19

Second Lesson - In his letter Peter extols the sacrifice of Christ as God's gift of immeasurable worth. 1 Peter 1:17-21

Gospel - The appearances of the Risen Christ bring surprise and joy. Luke 24:13-35

CALL TO WORSHIP

Leader: The grace of our Lord Jesus Christ be with you all.

People: And also with you.

Leader: Repent and be baptized, every one of you, in the name of Jesus the Messiah, for the forgiveness of your sins.

People: We will receive the gift of the Holy Spirit.

Leader: For the promise is to you and to your children

People: and to all who are far away, everyone whom the Lord our God may call.

INVOCATION

Limitless Giver, Anointed Benefactor, Anointing Spirit, we come to you in prayer together because you have reached out to baptize us and anoint us as your children. Receive our worship, which is worthy of you only as we are governed by the Spirit; through Jesus Christ our Lord. Amen

PRAYER OF CONFESSION

Truthful God, patient Teacher, Inspiration of prophets, we confess that we are often dull and sluggish in our thinking and slow of heart in believing. We prefer to hear what we already know than to think out something we have not heard before. We cherish our mixture of faith and doubt, rather than seek the surer faith that comes with a broader knowledge of the scriptures. Forgive our use of less than our full intellectual capacities in worship and less than an adventurous faith in following you; through Jesus Christ, fully human, fully divine. Amen

Declaration of Pardon

Pastor: Friends, hear the Good News! It was no perishable stuff, like gold or silver, that bought your freedom from the empty folly of your traditional ways.

People: The price was paid in precious blood, as it were of a lamb without mark or blemish—the blood of Christ.

Pastor: Friends, believe the Good News!

People: In Jesus Christ, we are forgiven.

[AND]

Exhortation

Fix your faith and hope in God, who raised Christ from the dead and gave him glory, the One who judges everyone impartially on the record of his or her deeds.

PRAYER OF THE DAY

Make yourself known to us again, risen Lord, in the breaking of the bread, so that every gathering of your people around your table may be a confirmation of the good news that you are alive from the dead and accompanying your people in the events of their journey. Amen

PRAYER OF THANKSGIVING

To know you, O God, is our joy. To be released from bondage to lesser "gods" is to be free to enjoy you anywhere and anytime. Our hearts exult in your love. Our spirit rejoices in communion with you. Our bodies are restful in the absence of fear when we remember your power over death. You lead us in the path of life. Your immediate presence will be fullness of joy. The honor you give is more pleasurable than earth's greatest tributes. Thanks is given to you, heavenly Parent, for giving the heavenly Son to the earthly death of the cross. Thanks is given to you, death-defying God, for raising Jesus of Nazareth from the dead, to prove that death could not keep him in its grip. Thanks is given to you, eternal Spirit, for inspiring our hope and our trust in you. Amen

PRAYER OF DEDICATION

Crucified-Jesus/Risen-Christ, your gift of baptism as a sacrament in the church makes simple washing with water the sign of forgiveness to the repentant and a gesture of acceptance to our children. Use us and our offerings to maintain the church and all your means of grace, in all the holy names of God. Amen

PRAYER OF INTERCESSION
AND COMMEMORATION

Holy God, you have built us like living stones into a spiritual house, to be a holy priesthood, to offer spiritual sacrifices acceptable to you through Jesus Christ. Hear our intercessions for his name sake.

As Jesus came to bring fire to the earth, kindle by the Holy Spirit holy fire in the church that all may see its light and be warmed by your love, fire which destroys evil but refines imperishable virtue. Use your church to save sinners, to lift up those who have been cast down, to enrich the poor, and feed the hungry. Establish the church as the Holy Way for all God's people so that no traveler, not even the simple, shall go astray. Confirm us in this mission knowing that whoever brings back a sinner from wandering will save the sinner's soul from death and will cover a multitude of sins.

God most high, be merciful to those in great sadness and laid aside by many sorrows, giving them rest and respite from their troubles. Heal the sick. Raise up the depressed. Send visitors to the lonely and the helpless.

Precious in your sight, Eternal God, is the death of your faithful ones. First, the death of your special child, Jesus, and then all who like him look for the resurrection like his to rise to eternal life in the home he has gone to prepare. As we give thanks for the lives of your faithful ones, undergird our faith by the strength of you Holy Spirit within us that we may bring glory to you, Eternal God, Immortal Son, and Loving Spirit. Amen

Fourth Sunday of Easter

First Lesson - Mutual sharing, as well as a common faith, is an essential factor in the growth of the infant church. Acts 2:42-47

Psalm 23

Second Lesson - Peter advises Christians that they can have God's approval for patience like that of Jesus when suffering unjustly. 1 Peter 2:19-25

Gospel - The shepherding of Jesus Christ is sincere caring and not hypocritical religious professionalism. John 10:1-10

CALL TO WORSHIP

Leader: The grace of our Lord Jesus Christ be with you all.
People: And also with you.
Leader: Hear the word of Jesus: I have come that you may have life and that you may have it in all its fullness.

People: Christ is the door; anyone who comes into the fold through him shall be safe.

INVOCATION

Creator of Life, Living Word of God, enlightening and enlivening Spirit, we come into your sanctuary through the door of Christ. In your presence we feel calm and safe because of the love you have offered all the world through Jesus Christ our Lord. Amen

PRAYER OF CONFESSION

Shepherd-God, who creates the fold: Shepherd-God, who goes out to seek the lost sheep: Shepherd-God, who draws the flock together: we have strayed like sheep and though you have brought us to your fold, we have not always followed in your steps. We may have begun to live the good life, but turn back too often to the old sinful life. We acknowledge the example Christ has set for us, but too rarely accepted the promised gifts of the Spirit to be like him. Forgive our wandering ways and grant us repentance and forgiveness for the sake of Jesus Christ, who suffered on our behalf. Amen

Declaration of Pardon

Pastor: Friends, hear the Good News! In his own person, Jesus carried our sins to the cross.

People: By his wounds we are healed.

Pastor: Friends, believe the Good News!

People: In Jesus Christ, we are forgiven.

[AND]

Exhortation

Repent and be baptized, everyone of you, in the name of Jesus the Messiah, for the forgiveness of sins; and you will receive the gift of the Holy Spirit. For the promise is to you and to your children and to all who are far away, everyone whom the Lord our God may call.

PRAYER OF THE DAY

Shepherd and Guardian of our souls, keep on calling us by name, so that we may not turn aside to follow the voice of anyone else who would destroy our faith and impoverish our life. Grant us fullness of life in your goodness and love unfailing. Amen

PRAYER OF THANKSGIVING

Good Shepherd, we rejoice in the bounteous provision you make us, so that we want nothing. We rest in the pleasant places life affords and in the peaceful times. We are thankful for the renewal of our life and strength. After struggle and weariness, even when life is dark and the shadow of death falls on us or those we love, you give us comfort and hope. When adversity closes us in, you send us surprises that fill our cup to overflowing. Your goodness and unfailing love will keep us in your household all the days of our lives, filled with praise and prayer. Amen

PRAYER OF DEDICATION

Divine Doorkeeper, receive our gifts and the witness of our words and lives, not only to keep these church doors open for us and our families, but to all whom you shall call into the company of faith and add to our number by baptism in the name of the Father, the Son, and the Holy Spirit. Amen

PRAYER OF INTERCESSION
AND COMMEMORATION

God most high, you have commanded us to pray no less for others than for ourselves. Hear our intercessions in the Name of your Son, Jesus Christ.

Bless the church and the people of Christ here and everywhere. Grant that all ministers and teachers of the gospel, being led by the Spirit, may lead others in the true and living way. As your Son Jesus, when he was in the world, was the light of the world, so now may the church be the light of the world, a city built on a hill that cannot be hid. In our individual lives may we follow the Christ in whom we profess to believe that as his disciples we may never walk in darkness but have by the Spirit the light of life.

Let that light shine also in our political activities, that we may influence government and public agencies toward justice and good faith so that our nation and the nations of the world may live together in mutual respect and peace.

Compassionate God, read the names written on our hearts, the members of our family and our friends for whom we are especially concerned. Hear our prayers for them and do for them as you know best. As faithful friends are life-saving medicine, send us also to those who are friendless and depressed. As you are everywhere present, stretch out your gentle hand to touch the sick in body and spirit. Relieve those in pain; strengthen those who are weak. Cheer those who are despairing, and give the dying sure hope in your promise of everlasting life.

Eternal God, we rejoice with those who have received their desire to depart and be with Christ, for that better life without sin and suffering. Bring us, in our own time, to the passage from life, through death, to that better life in sure and certain faith in the living Christ who promises to be with us always. And to you, Fatherly, Brotherly, Motherly God, be given all esteem and love by all your children on earth and in heaven. Amen

Fifth Sunday of Easter

First Lesson - Stephen becomes the first martyr of the church, with a Christ-like forgiving spirit witnessed by the Saul whose name will become Paul. Acts 7:55-60

Psalm 31:1-5, 15-16

Second Lesson - The Christian church is seen by Peter as a new tribe of priests or a new nation to bring light in a dark world. 1 Peter 2:2-10

Gospel - Jesus will lead us to a homeland being prepared for the family of God. John 14:1-14

CALL TO WORSHIP

Leader: The grace of our Lord Jesus Christ be with you all.

People: And also with you.

Leader: Come to the Lord, our living Stone—

People: the Stone rejected by many but choice and precious in the sight of God.

Leader: Come, and let yourselves be built as living stones into a spiritual temple.

People: We will become a holy priesthood, to offer spiritual sacrifices acceptable to God through Jesus Christ.

INVOCATION

Holy and Loving God, we come to you knowing that we will not be rejected because of our trust in Jesus Christ our Lord. We worship you for the grace you have offered us through him but also to intercede for the world that still rejects your Son. Hear our offerings of praise and petition through Jesus Christ our Savior. Amen

PRAYER OF CONFESSION

Invisible Father seen only in the visible Son, invisible Worker at work in Jesus of Nazareth, Divine Doer doing greater things still in those who have faith in you; forgive our failure to accomplish what you have wanted to do through us. Too often we have allowed our faith to grow weak, not sustaining it with honest questions addressed to you in your church and in your word. Like Thomas and Philip, we have had doubts out of a lack of understanding but not the same readiness to get our questions answered. Forgive our wandering, our fuzzy mindedness, our lack of vitality when you have given us Jesus to be for us the way, the truth, and the life. Amen

Declaration of Pardon

Pastor: Friends, hear the Good News! You are now the people of God, who once were not.

People: Once outside God's mercy, now we have received mercy.

Pastor: Friends, believe the Good News!

People: In Jesus Christ, we are forgiven.

[AND]

Exhortation

You are a people owned by God, to proclaim the triumphs of Christ, who has called you into marvelous light.

PRAYER OF THE DAY

Bring us to your house, heavenly Parent, trusting in your preparation to receive us, following Jesus who is the way, learning of Jesus who is the truth, drawing strength from Jesus who is the life. Amen

PRAYER OF THANKSGIVING

Light in darkness, Life out of death, Creator of unity, we rejoice in the triumphs of your love and grace. Out of darkness and doubt and distress you bring us to light and certainty and peace. Out of mortality and fear of death and unbelief, you lead us to trust and hope and eternal life. Out of scatteredness and shapelessness and clumsy purposelessness, you make us into a people, a worshipping community, a corporation for service; through Jesus Christ, Prince of Priests. Amen

PRAYER OF DEDICATION

Creator and Sustainer of the church, so keep us in the faith that we may not be separated from you and one another but united in a common service with diverse but complementary gifts to offer you, through Jesus Christ. Amen

PRAYER OF INTERCESSION
AND COMMEMORATION

Gracious God, as you have called us to make disciples of all nations—baptizing them in the name of the Father, and of the Son, and of the Holy Spirit—so we pray for the people of all nations, that they may come to you. Bless the preaching of the good news, that those who hear may believe and be baptized in your name and be added to the membership of your church.

Continue to provide gifts of healing to your church so that as the apostles healed in the name of Jesus Christ of Nazareth so today also the lame will walk and deaf hear and the mute speak to give praise to your holy name. In the congregation may the sick call for the elders of the church and have them pray over them, anointing them with oil in the name of the Lord. So may the prayer of faith save the sick— the Lord raise them up—and anyone who has committed sins be forgiven.

Father of us all, Brother of us all, Mother of us all, we rejoice that in your house there are many dwelling places. Jesus our brother has been raised from death to life and from life among us to prepare a place for us. We give thanks for the assurance through him that our loved ones who have departed this life are graciously received by you. Keep us strong in the faith so that when our time of death arrives we will depart with unshaken confidence in your care and custody of us through Christ our Savior. Amen

Sixth Sunday of Easter

First Lesson - Paul's preaching identifies God with the gospel of Christ's resurrection, sparking both curiosity and ridicule. Acts 17:22-31

Psalm 66:8-20

Second Lesson - Baptism saves us from sins in the present life for the life of the Spirit in heaven with the resurrected and ascended Christ. 1 Peter 3:13-22

Gospel - The Spirit of truth will counsel disciples after the resurrection of Jesus so that they are not alone but inspired to loving obedience of the continuing commands of the Risen Christ. John 14:15-21

CALL TO WORSHIP

Leader: The grace of our Lord Jesus Christ be with you all.

People: And also with you.

Leader: Come and see all that God has done, magnanimous in dealing with humanity. Come, listen, all who revere God.

People: We revere God, and will rehearse all God has done.

INVOCATION

With open eyes and alert ears we come to worship you, O God. Though it is in you we live and move and have our being, we can be unaware of you, without intending to be, in the course of the week. Renew our personal knowledge of you as we worship through Jesus Christ our Lord. Amen

PRAYER OF CONFESSION

Giver of commandments, we have received them but have not kept them wholly. Perfect Keeper of commandments, we have not loved fully as you love. Interpreter of commandments, we have resisted the truth, not wanting to know fully what you expect of us. Forgive incomplete obedience, half-hearted love, and evasion of the whole truth. We seek your mercy and counsel through Jesus Christ our Lord. Amen

Declaration of Pardon

Pastor: Friends, hear the Good News! Christ died for our sins once and for all. He, the just, suffered for the unjust, to bring us to God.

People: We reverence Christ in our hearts with deep gratitude and love.

Pastor: Friends, believe the Good News!

People: In Jesus Christ, we are forgiven.

[AND]

Exhortation

Hold the Lord Christ in reverence in your hearts. Always be ready with your defense whenever you are called to account for the hope that is in you, but make that defense with modesty and respect.

PRAYER OF THE DAY

Spirit of truth, grant us such further disclosures of the Father and the Son that we may be aware that God is with us and in us so that we may lovingly worship you and obey your commandments, even among those who do not receive you; through Jesus Christ, also our advocate with the Father. Amen

PRAYER OF THANKSGIVING

God everywhere, God with us, God in us, we may find you and know you anywhere. We are grateful that you give us life and breath, together with all human beings. We acknowledge your greatness in designing the world and creating boundaries of time and place. You display great patience with us in our times of ignorance and delay the day of judgement that we may rediscover you and our solidarity with all humanity. Most of all you have given us Jesus Christ, raised from the dead, to lead us to repentance and the full knowledge of who we are as offspring of the eternal. We worship you, O God, Creator, Judge, and Savior. Amen

PRAYER OF DEDICATION

Ruler of nations and peoples, Head of the church, Spirit of the church: we have vowed to give ourselves in every way as members of the body of Christ. We are here to fulfill our vows and to give substance to our promises. Receive us and our offerings for the strengthening of the church; through Jesus Christ our Lord. Amen

PRAYER OF INTERCESSION AND COMMEMORATION

We love you, Heavenly Parent, because you bend down to listen to us when we call. We come to you not only with our own entreaties but for our brothers and sisters as well.

We pray for your church universal. Fill it with all truth with all peace. Where it is corrupt, purge it. Where it is in error, direct it. Where it is superstitious, rectify it. Where it is right, strengthen and confirm it. Where it is in want, furnish it. Where it is divided and rent asunder, build it up in unity, God of Israel and the church.

God of creation, you visit the earth and water it, you greatly enrich it; you provide the people with grain, for so you have prepared it. The meadows clothe themselves with flocks; the valleys deck themselves with grain; they shout and sing together for joy. May there be abundance of grain in the land; may our orchards bear abundant fruit and our vineyards be heavy with grapes. May people blossom in our towns and cities as we clear the air. Bless all who farm and all who work for a healthier environment.

Compassionate God, hear our prayers for all who are troubled in mind and circumstance. Restore to health those who are sick and those recovering from surgery. May they, with new health and strength, come to your house to give thanks to you and for those who have cared for them.

Cheer the friendless, console the mourning, and receive the spirits of the dying through the mercy of our Lord Jesus Christ, crucified and risen from the dead.

Lord of heaven and earth, you do not live in shrines made by human hands, nor are your served by human hands, as though you need anything, since you give all mortals life and breath and all things. You have not left us to search for you, to grope for you, nor to find you by the art and imagination of mortals. You have appointed Jesus Christ to reveal yourself in both death and resurrection, and he has gone into heaven and is at your right hand. We rejoice in his victory over sin and death with the company of those who already surround your throne of grace. Deliver us from temptation and doubt, that at your call we may join that happy congregation in heaven with Jesus Christ, to whom, with you and the Holy Spirit, be ascribed glory and praise. Amen

Seventh Sunday of Easter

First Lesson - The clouds are a curtain brought down on the end of the final act of the earthly drama of Jesus of Nazareth. Acts 1:6-14

Psalm 68:1-10, 32-35

Second Lesson - Peter holds out the hope for us that after the ordeal of suffering will come exaltation as experienced by Jesus. 1 Peter 4:12-14; 5:6-11

Gospel - This climactic prayer of Jesus is for the unity of the apostles and the church to come. John 17:1-11

CALL TO WORSHIP

Leader: The grace of our Lord Jesus Christ be with you all.

People: And also with you.

Leader: Worship God, the sovereign Lawgiver of Sinai. Worship the One who ascends from the hill called Olive.

People: We receive the Spirit without whom we cannot truly worship.

INVOCATION

Prep. prayer
6/30/02 See below

We humble ourselves under your mighty hand, O God, that we may be exalted in due season. We seek your protection from the evil that is in the world and gather that we may find new guidance and inner discipline in the company of other Christians; through Jesus Christ our Lord. Amen

before you.

↓ healing, and strength

PRAYER OF CONFESSION

O God,

God of all grace, Christ of glory, powerful Spirit, we confess that the tempter sometimes catches us unawares. When things are going well for us, pride in our deserving such

↳we tend to forget you are our Creator and our loving Father.

6/30/02

prosperity may be the very cause of our downfall. When we are convinced that we can get by on our own, unexpected reverses can drag us down with anxiety. Then we are tempted to believe that you do not care and cannot bring us through our time of adversity. Restore, establish, and strengthen us in the faith of Jesus Christ. Amen

Declaration of Pardon

Pastor: Friends, hear the Good News! The Spirit of God is resting upon us.

People: The Spirit of God will give us cause for joy as we are willing to share the suffering of Christ.

Pastor: Friends, believe the Good News!

People: In Jesus Christ, we are forgiven.

[AND]

Exhortation

Humble yourselves under the almighty hand of God, who will lift you up in due time and cares for you always.

PRAYER OF THE DAY

Holy Parent, protect us as our Savior has prayed, that we may not seek independence, but unity, the unity of love and obedience, so that the world also may believe in the one you have sent, Jesus your Son. Amen

PRAYER OF THANKSGIVING

Great Sovereign over all the earth, you are high above the most powerful of earth's princes and mighty ones. We are grateful for our heritage of faith from the days of Abraham, to the apostle, to the present day. We are privileged to pray in the company of all the faithful in this and every generation. Though we are undeserving, we are honored to bear the name of Christ, having heard and heeded the good news of Jesus Christ. Receive our thanksgiving for all the prayers of

Christ and others for us and for the unity of your church, to the glory of your name. Amen

PRAYER OF DEDICATION

At prayer together before you, God of the gospel, we come as adults and children to obey the gospel and do the good to which you point us, moved by the Spirit to share the work and the suffering of Jesus Christ. Amen

PRAYER OF INTERCESSION AND COMMEMORATION

God of the ancients, Christ our contemporary, timeless Holy Spirit, hasten the day when the earth will be full of the knowledge of you as the waters cover the sea.

Bless every broadcast and telecast of the good news of Jesus Christ, that grace and truth may be shared by the listening public as well by those who hear your word in the gathering of your people in churches large and small. Give favor to all ministers of your Word and Sacraments that the means of grace may be available to people in urban and rural settings.

Bless all Bible societies that translate, publish, and distribute the written word of God through churches that worship in many hundreds of languages. Expedite the spread of the history of your saving acts to wherever people live. Bless all literacy volunteers who teach adults as well as children to read the Word of life and those who translate into writing the unwritten languages of primitive tribes so that they may hear the good news in their own language and respond in faith and thanksgiving.

In our daily lives may we carry faith to the doubting, hope to the fearful, strength to the weak-willed, and comfort to the bereaved. Speak through us your word of pardon to the guilty, a word of peace to the distraught, a word of reconciliation to those in conflict.

Remember for good our land and our leaders and our representatives to other nations. May we be instruments of your peace in an often angry world.

Bless all who care for our sick and aged, baby-sitters and teachers of preschool children, teachers of our young from kindergarten to university, that all may serve your highest purposes for all humanity.

Comfort, divine Spirit, all who mourn. To all whose day draws to an end, give light at evening time.

The memory of the righteous is a blessing, but the name of the wicked will fade away. We give thanks to you for the remembrance of those who have been our fathers and mothers and brothers and sisters in the faith, who are beyond the slight momentary afflictions of this life, having been prepared for an eternal weight of glory beyond all measure.

Keep us in spiritual readiness for continued communion with them now and in heaven with you, Fatherly, Brotherly, Motherly God, our love and our life. Amen

Pentecost

First Lesson - The Spirit of God bridges language barriers to begin the creation of one church for Jesus Christ. Acts 2:1-21

[OR]

The Spirit of God touches not only Moses but the seventy elders to the dismay of some others. Numbers 11:24-30

Psalm 104:1*a*, 24-34, 35*b*

Second Lesson - The inspiration of the Holy Spirit is essential to the confession of Jesus as Lord and the empowerment of the membership of the church. 1 Corinthians 12:3-13 or **Acts 2:1-21**

Gospel - The imagery of the river is used by Jesus to describe the outpouring of the Holy Spirit on all believers in him. John 7:37-39

CALL TO WORSHIP

Leader: The grace of our Lord Jesus Christ be with you all.

People: And also with you.

Leader: Sing to the Eternal One as long as you live.

People: We will praise our God while we have any breath.

INVOCATION

God our Creator, without air we could not breathe or speak. Without your Spirit we could not pray. While we live and breathe, we will sing our praise to you and invoke your name in our prayers; through Jesus Christ our Lord. Amen

PRAYER OF CONFESSION

Creator God, personal God, Giver of life, your works of nature are countless, your patience with mankind seems endless, your gifts of grace are various. We do not appreciate the wisdom of your creating genius without continued study and wonder. We take for granted too many of the creatures to which you have given life in our earth and sea and sky. We forget to give thanks and to bring praise to your name. We are jealous of the gifts you have given others and fail to use the particular gifts you have given us. Forgive the neglect of our gifts and of the opportunities to use them in the body of Christ, the church; through Jesus Christ our Lord. Amen

Declaration of Pardon

Pastor: Friends, hear the Good News! We were all brought into one body by baptism, in the one Spirit.

People: Whatever our language and nationality, whatever our place in society, that One Spirit was poured out for all of us to drink.

Pastor: Friends, believe the Good News!

People: In Jesus Christ, we are forgiven.

[AND]

Exhortation

There are a variety of gifts, but the same Spirit. There are varieties of service, but the same Lord. There are many forms of work, but all of them, in all, are the work of the same God. Use your gifts for some useful purpose.

PRAYER OF THE DAY

Holy Spirit, given One, gift of God, the Sender and the Sent, grant us continuing peace and the gift of discernment, that we may be as forgiving as you are and as true in expecting repentance in others as in ourselves. Amen

PRAYER OF THANKSGIVING

God of variety, we give thanks for your many and varied gifts to the church; for gifts of wise speech, putting deep knowledge into words; for gifts of faith and healing of mind and body; for the gifts of prophecy and discernment of truth and falsehood; for ecstatic speech and music and the ability to interpret it. We rejoice in the unity that is possible when these gifts are received willingly and coordinated by the Spirit as the activity of the one Body of Christ. We celebrate that unity of one Lord, one faith, one baptism, one work. May your glory stand forever, that you may rejoice in your own work in nature and in the church. Amen

PRAYER OF DEDICATION

God all glorious, there is nothing we can tell you that you do not know. There is nothing we can give you that you have not made possible. Though you have given us the freedom to be silent and to withhold our gifts, we offer our prayers and our gifts; in the name and spirit of Jesus Christ. Amen

PRAYER OF INTERCESSION
AND COMMEMORATION

Tireless God, you will satisfy the weary, and will replenish all who are faint. Revive your church by the energizing of the Holy Spirit, that when reviled, we may bless; when persecuted, we may endure; and not grow weary in doing what is right, to reap at harvest time, if we do not give up.

Uphold all who minister to your people in this and every land, in proclaiming the good news, teaching the young, visiting the needy, admonishing the erring, and in declaring the counsels and invitations of your word.

We pray for our country and its leadership. Raise up as our leaders persons who are after your own heart, not seekers after power, fame, or advantage for themselves, but such as are set to do your will, fearless and faithful for your honor.

We pray for our schools and colleges, that teachers and scholars may set your wisdom above all lesser learning. Rebuke pursuits of freedom that exploit the weak and the simple. Teach the discipline of loving the highest good and the equal rights of every neighbor.

We pray for our homes that they may be safe and loving for us and our children, a shelter from storm and strife, with open windows to heaven and open doors to welcome the stranger. Link our homes together into a chain of prayer that maintains the unity of the Spirit in the bond of peace.

Healing Spirit, inspire all caregivers who work with the poor, the sick, the addicted, the imprisoned. Bless chaplains in the armed forces and in hospitals and prisons. Send your people to befriend the lonely, to comfort the sorrowing, to cheer the depressed. Beyond all human agency do your own healing work in the hearts of all who look to you.

Helping Spirit and Comforter, support all penitents who falter in leaving their old ways to follow yours. Guide those who seem to find no human friend and feel unloved. Bring together those who can be mutually supportive. Grant peace and true freedom to those held captive by lust or any addiction.

Holy Father, Holy Brother, Holy Spirit, we are grateful that we are no longer strangers and aliens in the earth, but citizens with the saints and also members of your holy family. As we give thanks for those already with you in heaven, we ask your continued grace that we live worthy of our calling, marked with the seal of the promised Holy Spirit, the pledge of our inheritance toward redemption as your own people, to the praise of your glory. Amen

After Pentecost

Trinity Sunday

First Lesson - This is the beginning of the book of beginnings. Genesis 1:1–2:4

Psalm 8:1-9

Second Lesson - Paul sends closing greetings to the church at Corinth. 2 Corinthians 13:11-13

Gospel - Jesus gives his great commission to the eleven remaining disciples to insure continuity of the faith. Matthew 28:16-20

CALL TO WORSHIP

Leader: The grace of our Lord Jesus Christ be with you all.

People: And also with you.

Leader: Ascribe to the Lord the glory due to his name.

People: We bow down to the Lord in the splendor of holiness.

INVOCATION

6/30/02

God

~~Creator~~ of Light, Light of the World, Illumining Spirit, having seen the light in Jesus Christ, we come to ~~worship~~ you on the day of the week when Jesus was raised from death to life. Illumine your written word in our hearing so that our response may be genuine and dispel the darkness that remains with us; for the sake of Jesus Christ our Lord. Amen

PRAYER OF CONFESSION

God of love, Son of grace, Spirit of community, it is easier to recite the creed than to test our faith in the living of it. Self-examination can be painful, and we would rather not be put to the test. When we have seen that we are off the track, we do not readily mend our ways. We may exchange the kiss

118

of peace around your table, but we are not always as agreeable in committee meetings. We want to live in peace, but sometimes do so only by withdrawing from people with whom we disagree. Grant us your loving forgiveness, that we may be gracious to those with whom we differ and not break up the community you meant to be unified in the Spirit, for Jesus' sake. Amen

Declaration of Pardon

Pastor: Friends, hear the Good News! The Lord will give strength to his people.

People: The Lord will bless his people with peace.

Pastor: Friends, believe the Good News!

People: In Jesus Christ, we are forgiven.

[AND]

Exhortation

Mend your ways; agree with one another; live in peace; and the God of peace will be with you.

PRAYER OF THE DAY

Sovereign Lord of heaven and earth, reassure all doubtful disciples of your authority, that they may be obedient to their commission to call all nations to discipleship, baptizing in the name of the Father, the Son, and the Holy Spirit. Amen

PRAYER OF THANKSGIVING

We rejoice in the knowledge of you, O God, for you love righteousness and justice and your love unfailing fills the earth. Your plans will survive when the plans of nations come to nothing. We give thanks to you with all the musical arts we have mastered. They are but faint praise beside the music of the stars and the majesty of the seas. We stand in awe of the power of creation you have exercised in the scattering of the stars and the gathering of the seas. We are humbly grateful that you receive us as your people for the sake of Jesus Christ. Amen

PRAYER OF DEDICATION

Without the wisdom and fullness of the Spirit, your church, O God, cannot speak the Word and increase the number of disciples. Bless both those who give themselves to prayer and the ministry of the Word and those who are responsible for the distribution of the gifts we bring, through Jesus Christ our Lord. Amen

PRAYER OF INTERCESSION AND COMMEMORATION

Saving God, as you called your church to testify for you first in Jerusalem, then Samaria, and to bear witness also in Rome, so continue to send your church to the remotest human habitations on our planet. May the whole body of the church, joined and knit together by every ligament with which it is equipped, as each part is working properly, promote the body's growth in building itself up in love. May the whole world know that we are Christians by our love for one another. May the unbelieving and doubting be received as they seek faith by the hearing of your word, preached and demonstrated in holy and loving living.

Sovereign God, you rule above all. Bless all nations and their leaders that they may be wise to acknowledge that they are responsible to you for the use or abuse of power.

May virtue and peace everywhere prevail. Bless the United Nations, that this body of nations may promote respect for political, religious, and academic freedom; liberty of the individual conscience; and human rights for rich and poor alike. Teach the art of negotiation until nations shall not lift up the sword against nation neither shall they learn war any more.

Bless our families, young and old, gathered in households and scattered by duties and travel and vocation. Keep our children from harm and danger. May our nurture of them in home and church and school develop in them a love of beauty and truth in art and in life. May they behold the beauty of the Lord in the house of the Lord.

Jesus, Lord of life, who came among us that we may have life and have it abundantly, through the Spirit continue your ministry of doing good and healing the sick. Hear us as we name in our hearts those of our family and friends who most need your healing touch. Deliver those who are captive to addictions of mind and body. Save those who are trapped in destructive and abusive relationships. Send your disciples to those who are lonely and afraid.

We rejoice, O God, that you have a book of remembrance written before you of those who revered and thought on your name. We recall especially those dear to us who taught us to revere your name and love your word. Having looked to Jesus, whom they followed, may we never look back and become unfit for the kingdom of God. Keep us in the way everlasting by your guiding and sustaining Spirit. We praise your name, Fatherly, Brotherly, Motherly God, our salvation and destination. Amen

Proper 4 (May 29-June 4)

First Lesson - This is a story of judgment and salvation that will become a parable of the church. Genesis 6:11-22

Psalm 46

Second Lesson - Paul makes clear to the Romans that the good news is not that God is tolerant of moral negligence but that there is provision for salvation through faith. Romans 1:16-17, 3:22b-28 (29- 31)

Gospel - Jesus warns against hypocrisy, which will be exposed, the disastrous end of deceitful living. Matthew 7:21-29

CALL TO WORSHIP

Leader: The grace of our Lord Jesus Christ be with you all.
People: And also with you.
Leader: In this place of prayer let us invoke God by name,
People: that we may know God's gracious blessing.

INVOCATION

We come, O God, to hear again your word warning of judgment to come and to prepare ourselves for your proffered salvation in the ark of the church. We rejoice in our baptism, which is a sign of our salvation: through Jesus Christ our Lord. Amen

PRAYER OF CONFESSION

Truthful God, Liberating Christ, humbling Spirit, we confess that we have sinned and are deprived of the divine splendor. We are not nearly as good as we were meant to be. Both the law and the prophets have clarified your justice and your willingness to justify us as we accept the sacrificial death of Christ for our sins. We have no reason for self-righteous pride but should be humble in gratitude for your free grace. Overlook the sins of our past and any unjustified pride, for the sake of the liberating Christ, who is making us free. Amen

Declaration of Pardon

Pastor: Friends, hear the Good News! All are justified by God's free grace alone, through his act of liberation in the person of Christ Jesus.

People: For God designed him to be the means of expiating sin by his sacrificial death, effective through faith.

Pastor: Friends, believe the Good News!
People: In Jesus Christ, we are forgiven.

[AND]

Exhortation

Do not brag about keeping the commandments. Justification by faith excludes such pride.

PRAYER OF THE DAY

Lord Jesus Christ, let us not call you Lord in vain but both hear and act on the words you speak so that our lives may be firmly founded on the rock of God's will and indestructible in the midst of the storms of life. Amen

PRAYER OF THANKSGIVING

Heavenly Parent, God of our ancestors, we thank you for all our fathers and mothers in the faith, natural parents and adopting parents, foster parents, and others who have been significant in the shaping of our minds and feelings, our ideas and our values, our goals and our behavior. We are grateful for the learning experiences that have strengthened our faith, memories that draw us to your house and to other places hallowed by awareness of your presence, occasions of sympathy and understanding too intimate to explain. We celebrate every home marked with signs of your faithful love, not only with art and symbol, but also with hospitality and human caring. Your truth is our foundation rock; your unfailing love, our shelter; your will, the walls that guard our way of life. All praise to you, God of all lands, all people, our people. Amen

PRAYER OF DEDICATION

We can only present what you freely give, gracious God. We express our faith and our thanksgiving in these offerings, that the church may continue to witness your justice, through the law, the prophets, and the gospel of your liberating son, Jesus Christ. Amen

PRAYER OF INTERCESSION
AND COMMEMORATION

Universal God, we pray that your way may be known upon earth, your saving power among all nations. Remember in blessing your whole church, granting it purity of life and doctrine, in purity peace, in peace unity, and in unity strength.

Remember this land that we love. Guide those who pilot the ship of state amidst treacherous waters. May your law be their chart and your guidance their pilot. Prosper every good venture and lawful enterprise.

Bless every effort to save people from wicked neighborhoods, unjust conditions, and the violence of the vicious. Save us from irreverence and godless philosophies that excuse human tyranny. As we learn to love you with all that we are and our neighbor as ourselves, may we share honestly and joyfully the bounty you have given us to be sufficient for everyone.

O Lord, by your life all people live, and trusting you is the life of the human spirit. Restore to health any who have made unhealthy choices in life and need to undo the damage they have done to their own bodies. Guide us in our daily decisions to care for our bodies and by our prayers to live abundantly the life of the spirit.

Guide those doing research into the unknown causes of many of our diseases, that both hereditary and environmental illnesses and disabilities may be treated and prevented. Bless and heal those who even now are looking to us for our prayers.

Strengthen the bonds of the covenant that bind us to one another in families, whether close or distant from each other. May our faith in the Lord Jesus save us and our households however scattered from us and from the house of prayer where they were baptized into the family of God.

We rejoice in the companionship of saints when we surround the table you have set in the church. May our communion with you at the holy table confirm the ties that bind together your people in heaven and earth. Keep us in faithful remembrance of the offering of himself by Jesus the Christ.

These our prayers we present before your throne of grace through the same Jesus Christ our Lord, to whom, with you and the Holy Spirit, be the glory both now and for ever. Amen

Proper 5 (June 5-11)

First Lesson - Abram is called out to begin a faith journey that will make of him and Sarai his wife a great nation to bring blessing to all nations favorable to them and their descendants. Genesis 12:1-9

Psalm 33:1-12

Second Lesson - Paul explains how Abraham is deserving of the title father of the faithful. Romans 4:13-25

Gospel - Jesus is not fussy, like the Pharisees, about the company he keeps but willingly brings God's grace to sinners. Matthew 9:9-13, 18-26

CALL TO WORSHIP

Leader: The grace of our Lord Jesus Christ be with you all.

People: And also with you.

Leader: Sing to the Eternal One as long as you live;

People: We will praise our God while we have any breath.

INVOCATION

Loving God, having been set free, we worship readily and not under compulsion. Receive our petitions and our praise, our intercessions for the world you love and for which you gave your Son, Jesus Christ our Lord. Amen

PRAYER OF CONFESSION

v|o 2

God of life, God of healing, ~~God of health~~, though we are reluctant to say that there is no health in us, we do confess that we are not in perfect spiritual health. We are grateful that Jesus came to ~~call bad characters, as a doctor is sent~~ to heal the sick. Save us from the pride that prevents our taking all the prescriptions of ~~this~~ healer ~~of the soul~~, Jesus of Nazareth. ~~Teach us also what it means to be merciful, that we may not shun the company of less discreet sinners in the church.~~ Be our healer until we ~~at last attain spiritual wholeness. Amen~~

and wounded
God of health
our
are made whole

Declaration of Pardon

Pastor: Friends, hear the Good News! Jesus said, I did not come to invite virtuous people, but sinners.

People: We come at the invitation of Jesus.

Pastor: Friends, believe the Good News!

People: In Jesus Christ, we are forgiven.

[AND]

Exhortation

As he said to Matthew, so Jesus says to you: "Follow me."

PRAYER OF THE DAY

Good Teacher, send us among those who need to hear your invitation to discipleship, that we may share the good news and express your mercy toward all sinners. Amen

PRAYER OF THANKSGIVING

God of Abraham and Sarah, we rejoice in your promises. Through them, father and mother of many nations, we have come to inherit the gift of faith in you, who makes the dead live and summons things that are not yet in existence as if they already were. We thank you for Jesus our Lord, whom you raised from the dead, for he was given up to death for our misdeeds and raised up to new life to justify us. Your promises to us are a matter of sheer grace, which we receive by faith and not by upholding the law. We honor you, O God, for freely justifying us. We call you Lord, Jesus Christ, for your death and resurrection. We receive you, divine Spirit, as an undeserved gift of eternal life. Amen

PRAYER OF DEDICATION

Gracious God, the death of Christ on the cross precludes any offering for our sins. Receive what we give and our promised service as a response in thanksgiving, through Jesus Christ, Lamb of God, Savior of the world. Amen

PRAYER OF INTERCESSION
AND COMMEMORATION

Your eyes, O Lord, are on the righteous, and your ears are open to their prayer. Your face is against those who do evil. Cleanse us by your Holy Spirit that we may be worthy to intercede for the world sometimes indifferent toward you.

Wisdom is a reflection of eternal light, a spotless mirror of your working, O God. Sanctify your church that it may bear a likeness of your goodness. Continue to use your people, not only in working out their own salvation with deep humility and reverence, but as co-laborers with Christ in your saving work. May the lowly be raised up and the old made new by the creating and renewing Spirit.

127

Revitalize your people in every land to be faithful and true to Christ and his cause, that the church may stem the tide of unbelief and blasphemy in the world and recruit the young to follow him. Recall those who have been led astray to walk again in the way that leads to life.

Bless this congregation and all its members that we may be resolute in our commitment to follow Christ both in common worship and in our private affairs.

Bless our country and our leaders. Grant gifts of prudence, courage, and strength that we may be led to follow policies that are equitable and that honor all people.

Watchful Parent in heaven, tend your sick children, rest the weary, soothe the suffering, comfort the dying. Send your children to brothers and sisters who are alone and needing caring company.

What no eye has seen, nor ear heard, nor the human heart conceived, you have prepared, O God, for those who love you. Ever keep us in that love so that we may be in communion with you and all your people in this world and the next and come to them and you at last, never to be separated again by misunderstanding or disagreement. To you, O God, be ascribed all paternal power, all brotherly affection, and all motherly love, as One God forever. Amen

Proper 6 (June 12-18)

First Lesson - Abraham and Sarah are hosts to God's messengers who renew the promise of a son who will be the beginning of a great nation. Genesis 18:1-15 (21:1-7)

Psalm 116:1-2, 12-19

Second Lesson - Paul does not promise that salvation spares us from suffering but that God can use that experience to enhance our character as Christians. Romans 5:1-8

Gospel - Jesus outlines a rigorous discipline for his disciples. Matthew 9:35-10:23

CALL TO WORSHIP

Leader: The grace of our Lord Jesus Christ be with you all.
People: And also with you.
Leader: Let us exult in God through our Lord Jesus Christ, through whom we have been granted reconciliation,
People: proving God's love for us sinners.

INVOCATION

In you, O God, we exult, for you have proved your love for us sinners in the life and death and resurrection of Jesus Christ. Receive our worship offered through the communion of the Holy Spirit with us and between us. Amen

PRAYER OF CONFESSION

Creator of the way, Finder of the lost, Guide of the trusting, we confess that we are helpless to save ourselves, that we have been willful and have left the way even when we have seen it clearly, that we have harassed others as they have harassed us, that self-control might have spared us some of our illnesses, and that our weaknesses can be overcome only by the health and strength you can give in spirit and soul and body. Forgive our sins. Heal our diseases. Have pity on us as did Jesus of Nazareth. Amen

Declaration of Pardon

Pastor: Friends, hear the Good News! God has shown us how much he loves us.
People: It was while we were yet sinners that Christ died for us.
Pastor: Friends, believe the Good News!

129

People: In Jesus Christ, we are forgiven.

[AND]

Exhortation

Rejoice in God through our Lord Jesus Christ, who has now made us God's friends.

PRAYER OF THE DAY

Patient Leader, help us to know our best skills, that we may find the place of greatest usefulness to people in need and so extend your ministry of love and healing and spread the good news of the kingdom. Name us and number us also among your disciples. Amen

PRAYER OF THANKSGIVING

Loving God, dying Son, living Lord, how amazingly you prove your love for us! Though you might have cast us off forever in anger at our sins, you show your loving forgiveness in the death of your Son and our Lord, Jesus Christ. We rejoice in the sacrificial death that saves us and the ongoing life that intercedes for us. We are filled with joyful trust and thanksgiving that you have befriended us. Weak and unworthy as we are, we thank you for your love. You are worthy of all praise, critical but conciliatory God, human and divine Christ, holy and hopeful Spirit. Amen

PRAYER OF DEDICATION

Good Lord, your love is everlasting and your constancy endures to all generations. Our gifts are limited and our vices will fade, but we want our children and our grand-children to worship you in gladness in this place; through Jesus Christ our Lord. Amen

PRAYER OF INTERCESSION
AND COMMEMORATION

Omnipresent God, we pray for the coming of the time of universal restoration that you announced long ago through your holy prophets. So also we pray that times of refreshing may come from your presence and that the Spirit's presence in the church may be more manifest in the world to the glory of the name of Jesus Christ our Lord. As in heaven the prayers of the saints are brought beore you as golden bowls full of incense, so may your church encircle with a golden chain of prayer the world you love and for which you gave your Son Jesus in poverty and death. Grant zeal to your church in telling the generous act of our Lord Jesus Christ, that though he was rich, yet for our sakes he became poor, so that by his poverty we might become rich. Through your church enrich the poor of the world with this great treasure of your grace.

As you have promised, dwell with your people, O God. Be light, joy, and peace in them by the Spirit that our homes may be rich in your wisdom, fragrant with prayer, and full of the music of praise. May our children grow up in the love that flows from you that knowing you, the Source of life and love, they may tap that resource all their lifetime.

We pray that you will heal and restore the sick, especially those we name in the silence of our hearts. Be near to all who mourn, and in their bereavement be their comfort and hope. Defend the innocent, deliver the tempted, and rescue those entraped by evil and addiction. Let no trial of faith shake or embitter your children, but bring them through their ordeal purified and made stronger in their trust in you.

Eternal God, your perfect Son Jesus shared our flesh and blood, so that through death he might destroy the one who has the power of death, that is, the devil. We rejoice in the faith of those who already have been received victorious in heaven through his victory. Grant that, persevering in our trust in the Risen Christ, we may enter into that triumph over sin and death and follow them into your heavenly glory.

131

To you, Father, Son, Holy Spirit, one God, be ascribed all majesty and conquest over evil, now and forever. Amen

Proper 7 (June 19-25)

First Lesson - That human rejection does not mean divine rejection is illustrated by the story of Hagar and her son. Genesis 21:8-21

Psalm 86:1-10, 16-17

Second Lesson - Paul writes of our baptism into the death and resurrection of Christ Jesus. Romans 6:1-11

Gospel - Jesus instructs the disciples of their place in the scheme of things, the limits of their dignity but also its promise. Matthew 10:24-39

CALL TO WORSHIP

Leader: The grace of our Lord Jesus Christ be with you all.

People: And also with you.

Leader: Come and bow down before God, and glorify God's name.

People: For God is great and does wondrous things; who alone is God.

INVOCATION

You alone are our God, and we will worship no one and nothing else. We give thanks for the good things you have done for us and all your people. We ask you to receive our praise and our petitions through Jesus Christ our Lord. Amen

PRAYER OF CONFESSION

Meticulous God of immeasurable grace, how shall we measure our sins? Only you know their real dimensions; the history of human disobedience; the ramifications of hatred; the multiplication of wrongdoing by generations; the perpetuation of prejudices by unthinking repetition; the aggravation of offenses by the unforgiving and vengeful. However you account for our sin, there are none of us who do not stand in need of some measure of your grace, which in Jesus Christ is out of all proportion to human wrongdoing. Amen

Declaration of Pardon

Pastor: Friends, hear the Good News! God's act of grace is out of all proportion to human wrongdoing.

People: God's gift has come to so many by the grace of the one man, Jesus Christ.

Pastor: Friends, believe the Good News!

People: In Jesus Christ, we are forgiven.

[AND]

Exhortation

Do not fear those who kill the body but cannot kill the soul. Fear him rather who is able to destroy both soul and body in hell.

PRAYER OF THE DAY

Creator of all life, reassuring Parent, help us to tell simply and clearly the promises of your love and care that we have received in secret so that our brothers and sisters who live in doubt and fear may trust you as well, through Jesus Christ our Lord. Amen

PRAYER OF THANKSGIVING

We give thanks to you, O God, that the gate of heaven may be found in any place, and your house wherever we receive your revelation. You send your messengers to us in both waking and sleeping hours, to comfort and reassure us of your constant care and love. You reaffirm to us promises old and new, in law and gospel, in Word and Sacrament. Receive our praise, Guardian of sparrows and of sinners, Teacher of the simple, Enlightener of all who seek light in darkness. Amen

PRAYER OF DEDICATION

Though we are bound to serve you, divine Master, we do not serve you without fault. Achieve your purposes through the church, despite our imperfect commitment to service and the reproach of the world, to the glory of your name. Amen

PRAYER OF INTERCESSION
AND COMMEMORATION

Compassionate God, may the offering of this ministry of intercession overflow with many thanksgivings to you. May we not only offer our prayers but contribute to the needs of the saints and extend hospitality to strangers.

Risen and glorious Christ, your eyes are like a flame of fire, to search out and refine your church of the dross that corrupts her life. Save your church from the sloth of indifference, from compromise with half-truths, from the influence of false leaders, from alliance with partisan political parties. May your light shine in the church like the morning star and offer hope of a better day.

Bless our land and counsel our leaders, our lawmakers, and all who administer the affairs of state. In our various vocations make us trustworthy and loyal to the crown of Christ.

To your tender care we commend all who are in sorrow, trouble, sickness, or want, remembering especially those who are not worshiping with us, as they usually do, because of failing health. Sustain all who look after the sick and bless all chaplains and church visitors who attend them in hospitals and nursing homes.

Deliver the dying from this body of death through Jesus Christ that all who trust in him and look for his appearing may know the joy of seeing him face to face.

Eternal God, we rejoice that the ransomed of the LORD have returned and come to the heavenly Zion with singing; they have obtained joy and gladness, and sorrow and sighing have flown away. In your own time bring us at last to the place you have prepared for us that there may be a joyful homecoming and a glad reunion with our beloved dead who have preceded us to behold your glory. To you, O God, we ascribe majesty, grace, and immeasurable love, now and ever. Amen

Proper 8 (June 26-July 2)

First Lesson - The near sacrifice of Isaac is a test of Abraham's faith in the face of the death of his only heir. Genesis 22:1-14

Psalm 13

Second Lesson - The dominion of sin is to be overturned by our willingness to be tools in God's hands to do what is right. Romans 6:12-23

Gospel - Jesus promises rewards for the smallest service to one of his prophets. Matthew 10:40-42

CALL TO WORSHIP

Leader: The grace of our Lord Jesus Christ be with you all.

People: And also with you.

Leader: Rejoice in your salvation.

People: We will sing to God who has dealt bountifully with us.

INVOCATION

Bountiful God, we voice our gratitude in prayer and song and the offering of ourselves in dedication to your church. You are saving us from our sins as we trust in Jesus Christ our Savior and worship in the Spirit. Amen

PRAYER OF CONFESSION

Perfect Parent, worthy Son, uniting Spirit, our love for you is not as worthy of you as it should be. Other loves compete in us for our response to your grace. Our feet have been set upon a new path of life through our baptism into Christ. We admit that we stray from that way, returning to the ways of death that should be left behind. We presume upon your grace by our sinning rather than draw upon the new life that is available to us in union with Christ Jesus. Forgive us for allowing your life and love to go so unrequited, for the sake of your devoted Son, Jesus Christ. Amen

Declaration of Pardon

Pastor: Friends, hear the Good News! Remember that in baptism we were baptized into the death and resurrection of Jesus Christ,

People: so that we may no longer be the slaves of sin, but alive to God.

Pastor: Friends, believe the Good News!

People: In Jesus Christ, we are forgiven.

[AND]

Exhortation

Set your feet upon the new path of life in the company of Jesus, and leave behind the old ways of sin and death.

PRAYER OF THE DAY

Divine-Human Cross-bearer and Leader, lead us away from goals that have been set by our families or ourselves, goals that are short of your purposes for us and for your whole family, that we may be worthy disciples and cross-bearers, for your sake. Amen

PRAYER OF THANKSGIVING

Maker of covenants, we are grateful for your generous Spirit in condescending to be partners with us in human governments and enterprises. Death-accepting, to-life-returning Christ, we are thankful for the baptism you share with us that we may know the splendor that lies beyond the dominion of sin and death. Giver of rewards, we are undeserving of the attention you give to the simplest acts of humanity and generosity. We are thankful for all the promises you have made and kept, and live in hope of the completion of the new creation you have undertaken as the kingdom of Jesus Christ. Amen

PRAYER OF DEDICATION

Divine Overseer, if even a cup of water for one of your disciples does not go unnoticed, then our offerings to support your ministers and the work of your church will also be rewarded. Grant us also the share of the prophet's reward and the blessing that comes in the company of good people.

PRAYER OF INTERCESSION
AND COMMEMORATION

Christ of glory, in your right hand are the stars of the churches. Save your people from having but the name of being alive. Arouse the slothful and confirm the faithful. Strengthen the good things that could die out, and may the work of your church stand the fire of testing. May your people hold fast to the truth that they have received in Christ and not defile the white robes of their baptism by disobedience to your directions.

God of the old and the young and those of middle years, may our children early come to you in faith and lifelong commitment. Sustain those who bear the burden and the heat of the day, all who must carry another's burdens as well as their own. Grant patience to those whose days are numbered, who have completed their working days and can only anticipate the service of heaven. Give them rest from their labors and an assured entry into heaven where their deeds follow them.

Enable us to keep the faith and continue their labors in the gospel while there is still time for us. To you we will come and experience a joyful reunion with our family in the household of God. And to you, O God, Father, Brother, Mother, we ascribe glory and praise, time without end. Amen

Proper 9 (July 3-9)

First Lesson - The arrangement of the marriage of Isaac to Rebekah is made by Abraham through an emissary. Genesis 24:34-38, 42-49, 58- 67

Psalm 45:10-17

Second Lesson - Paul describes the conflict within us as between the old and the new nature. Romans 7:15-25

Gospel - Jesus describes the contradictions in the behavior of his critics and his happiness at the response of the simple-hearted. Matthew 11:16-19, 25-30

CALL TO WORSHIP

Leader: The grace of our Lord Jesus Christ be with you all.
People: And also with you.
Leader: Hear the invitation of Jesus: Come to me, all those
      whose work is hard, whose load is heavy; and I
      will give you relief.

People: **We will bend our necks to your yoke and learn from you, for you are gentle and humble-hearted.**
Leader: Your souls will find relief.
People: **For his yoke is good to bear, and his load is light.**

INVOCATION

Compassionate Christ, we have come to learn from you who are gentle and humble in heart. As we seek to emulate you in our worship, prepare us for your service as true and loyal companions. Amen

PRAYER OF CONFESSION

Creative Spirit, you have made us in your likeness, male and female and have made marriage one of the covenants through which you make families and nations. We have broken such covenants with impunity and failed to practice the true mutuality that is the grace of a good marriage. Forgive such dishonor and the abuse of family ties. Teach us to find our place in your scheme of things whether in marriage or celibacy like your Son, Jesus of Nazareth. Amen

Declaration of Pardon

Pastor: Friends, hear the Good News! God alone frees us from the rule of sin in our own natures.
People: **God alone frees us from sin in our own natures, through Jesus Christ.**
Pastor: Friends, believe the Good News!
People: **In Jesus Christ, we are forgiven.**

[AND]

Exhortation

Learn from Jesus, who is gentle and humble-hearted, and you will find that working with him is comfortable and not too difficult.

PRAYER OF THE DAY

Ruler of heaven and earth, disclose to us in our simplicity all we need to know of your judgement, that we may not carry loads of guilt too heavy for us to bear but, experiencing your forgiveness and relief, may serve easily in the light yoke with Jesus Christ. Amen

PRAYER OF THANKSGIVING

You are our Creator and Helper, O God. When illness or accident have endangered our lives, we have been spared, and life seems more precious to us. When our lives have been extended and we sense their value, we have committed ourselves to your service with new sincerity and energy. We are grateful that we do not serve you alone, but may enjoy the company and support of others, and especially the nearness of our yokefellow, Jesus Christ. Amen

PRAYER OF DEDICATION

Master Worker, we bend our necks to your yoke and will learn to serve with you as you teach us. Use us and all that is ours to accomplish, with humility and good humor, the high purposes of your church, to the glory of your name. Amen

PRAYER OF INTERCESSION
AND COMMEMORATION

Founder of all nations, from one ancestor you have made all nations to inhabit the whole earth and allotted the times of their existence and the boundaries of the places where they would live. It is appropriate then for us to pray to you not only for ourselves in this place but for all your family of nations everywhere.

Your church has found in many places a wide door for effective work has opened, but still there are many adversaries. We pray especially for the church which struggles to exist where hampered by legal restrictions to receive new members. Increase religious liberties everywhere in the world so that faith will be free and the whole truth be sought. Save us from seeking to compel the faith of any and to deny the power of the truth in itself.

May our leaders seek always to be servants of the truth and justice and not captive to the greed of interest groups high or low. Bless and prosper our country in the family of all nations that we may share what we have with others as we receive what others have to share with us. Grant us a true appreciation of the best gifts that every nation has to offer, and save our world from overblown nationalisms and fanatic religions and political prejudices.

Remind us, heavenly Parent, that you treat us like children; for what child is there whom a parent does not discipline? So may we endure trials for the sake of discipline, knowing that you have not forsaken us. There is no testing overtaken us that is not common to everyone. You are faithful and will not let us be tested beyond our strength, but with the testing will also provide the way out so that we may be able to endure it.

Compassionate Savior, recover those who have strayed from your church and are captive in the snares of evildoers. In the far country of their dissolution may they come to themselves and to you and be truly saved.

We commend to you, O God, those dear to us who are leaving this life, prepared to be received into the inheritance among all who are sanctified. Grant us the fullness of your Holy Spirit that we may also be built up in the faith, in the fullness of your grace in Christ Jesus, to be received at last into your presence with ultimate joy. To you, our God, we give praise and endless thanksgiving. Amen

Proper 10 (July 10-16)

First Lesson - The struggle of twins, Jacob and Esau, which began in the womb of Rebekah, is consumated in the over-turning of the birthright in a moment of weakness. Genesis 25:19-34

Psalm 119:105-112

Second Lesson - Beyond our freedom from sin and guilt, says Paul, is the empowerment to live in peace with God. Romans 8:1-11

Gospel - When Jesus begins teaching with parables, he gives the disciples an example of how to interpret them. Matthew 13:1-9, 18-23

CALL TO WORSHIP

Leader: The grace of our Lord Jesus Christ be with you all.

People: And also with you.

Leader: Pray as a little child. The Spirit who adopts us as children of God enables us to pray with confidence to our heavenly Parent.

People: We will pray with all the ease and familiarity of small children to earthly parents.

INVOCATION

"Gentle Jesus, meek and mild, Look upon a little child;
Pity my simplicity, Suffer me to come to thee."
Heav'nly Parent, hear my prayer, Grant me only what is fair As to others you would give: Life eternal let me live.
Holy Spirit, fresh'ning wind, Blow away all thoughts of sin, Mind of Christ within me leave; Childlike innocence re-trieve." Amen (First two stanzas, Charles Wesley, "Gentle Jesus, Meek and Mild"; additional stanzas by the author.)

PRAYER OF CONFESSION

Persistent Word-Creator, patient Teacher, persuasive Spirit, you are tireless in speaking to us, but we find it easy to close our minds, to refuse to hear what would require painful change, to reject the truth because it is inconvenient. Forgive deliberate denseness of mind, fearful resistance to change, stubborn insistence that our way is the best way. Continue your speaking until we hear. Try new parables on us until we think and understand. Argue with us until we do your will. What else will your love in Christ allow you to do? Amen

Declaration of Pardon

Pastor: Friends, hear the Good News! All who are moved by the Spirit of God are children of God.

People: We are heirs of God's splendor with Jesus Christ.

Pastor: Friends, believe the Good News!

People: In Jesus Christ, we are forgiven.

[AND]

Exhortation

Do not be content simply to do what comes naturally. Live on the spiritual level as a Christian in whom Christ dwells by the Spirit.

PRAYER OF THE DAY

God of mystery, Sharer of Divine Secrets, Spirit of God's whole family, enable us to hear what you speak, to see what you disclose, to respond as to a parent in our prayers, that we may be strengthened to share the suffering of Christ, our brother, and live free from fear until the day of splendor comes. Amen

PRAYER OF THANKSGIVING

Creator of the visible and the invisible, divine Deliverer, Life-sustaining Spirit, all that is depends upon you and rejoices in your praise. You blot out our sins and free us to live as your children in love and helpfulness. Your Spirit both inspires our prayers and promotes our growth in Christ. All whom you deliver from sin and death praise you in your household. We especially rejoice in the reassuring voice of the Spirit, calling us into one loving family with you, Father, Son, and Mothering Spirit. Amen

PRAYER OF DEDICATION

Holy Parent, you relieve us from the burden of our guilt and save us from the loneliness that isolates us from others and from you. With these our offering, we pledge our vows of service in the company of this holy family, in the spirit of Jesus Christ. Amen

PRAYER OF INTERCESSION
AND COMMEMORATION

With our voices we cry to you, O LORD; with our voices we make supplication to you, O LORD. We pour out our complaints before you; we tell our troubles before you and the adversities of our world.

Grant to your church the compassionate spirit of Jesus who saw many people, harassed and helpless, like sheep without a shepherd. As we have enjoyed comfort and care in your congregation, may we welcome strangers and foreigners into our company that they may share your grace and the sacraments of your church. Send us to those who have been scattered that they may be returned to your fold and to the lost that they may find themselves and commit themselves to your keeping.

Continue to us, generous God, the blessings of your providence in our land. Deliver us from the godless and self-seekers and raise up as our leaders the reverent and seekers for truth and justice. Overrule unrighteous schemes, and teach us to find the truth in controversies, that in negotiation we may find what is just, loving mercy and walking humbly before you and before one another.

Mortal but eternal Christ, you shared our humanity and know human weakness and strength. Hear our prayers for the sick and the aged. As their days shorten, so let their strength be lengthened. Encourage the depressed; give joy to those who are sad and sorrowing; strengthen the resistance of those who are tempted to evil; grant your grace to those who have fallen and lift them up again. Give peace to the dying and light at eventide.

Like a haven for a ship saved from a storm, O God, you have brought our beloved dead to their desired haven in heaven. Bring us at last out of all our distress, stilling the storms that assail us and the waves that go over us that we may share the gladness of their peace and quiet and with them give thanks to you for your steadfast love and your wonderful works for all humanity.

We will praise your hallowed name, Fatherly, Brotherly, Motherly God. Amen

Proper 11 (July 17-23)

First Lesson - The dream of Jacob will be identified for thousands of years as Jacob's ladder. Genesis 28:10-19

Psalm 139:1-12, 23-24

Second Lesson - Paul defines our relationship with God through the Holy Spirit as that of adopted children. Romans 8:12-25

Gospel - Matthew continues his reporting of the parables Jesus told in preaching to and teaching the multitudes and also gives the follow-up explanation to the disciples. Matthew 13:24-30, 36-43

CALL TO WORSHIP

Let us bless God from our innermost hearts, forgetting none of the benefits of God's compassion: pardon for our guilt, healing for our suffering, constant love, and renewal of our strength.

[OR]

Leader: The grace of our Lord Jesus Christ be with you all.

People: And also with you.

Leader: Let us bless God from our innermost hearts, forgetting none of the benefits of God's compassion.

People: Let us bless God for God's pardon for our guilt,

Leader: God's healing for our suffering,

People: God's constant love and renewal of our strength.

INVOCATION

We bless you, O God, in all sincerity for the many benefits you have granted to us. In Christ we are rich indeed. Your Spirit is poured out in generous measure on your church. Receive the worship we offer you in the Spirit, through Jesus Christ our Lord. Amen

PRAYER OF CONFESSION

God of long range planning, God involved in human history, God who saves us in hope, we confess that we are impatient with your timing. We want immediate judgement on the sins of others, though not on our own. The time of our own suffering seems endless, but the duration of deprivation for others we can shrug off. We want instant recognition of our achievements but are jealous of the honors afforded others. Forgive the pride that proposes that we know better than you do what should be done and when, for the sake of Jesus of Nazareth, who also struggled against doing your will but did it nevertheless. Amen

Declaration of Pardon

Pastor: Friends, hear the Good News! We have been saved, though only in hope.

People: The splendor is still in store for us.

Pastor: Friends, believe the Good News!

People: In Jesus Christ, we are forgiven.

[AND]

Exhortation

Endure suffering and frustration in hope of entering into the liberty and splendor of the children of God.

PRAYER OF THE DAY

Nourish our hopes with prophetic promises, eternal God, that our timeline may be synchronized with yours, as was the earthly time of your Son, Jesus Christ. Amen

PRAYER OF THANKSGIVING

Obscure God, disclosed through a strange history and a suffering Son of an insignificant nation, we stand in awe of your ways. You bring to power the powerless and overthrow the tyrant. You are compassionate and gracious, showing your favor to slaves as well as sovereigns, promising liberty to all who live in hope of the final triumph of your goodness. In a blighted world we rejoice in the firstfruits that point to a final harvest still to come. In mortality we wait with eager anticipation for the freedom of immortality. We praise you, God of creation, God of resurrection, God of restoration. Amen

PRAYER OF DEDICATION

Multiplier of small things, make of us a force for good, uplifting what is best in our community, to the glory of your name and the growth of your rule in the world. Amen

PRAYER OF INTERCESSION AND COMMEMORATION

Divine Redeemer, though we may not rejoice in sufferings for your sake or in reality complete what is lacking in your afflictions for the sake of your body, the church, at least may we enter into your ministry of reconciliation for which you gave yourself in death and resurrection.

Hear us as we pray for the church, holy, catholic, and apostolic, of which, by your grace, we are members. Remove the errors and divisions that disturb and weaken the church. Raise up a continuing succession of faithful ministers to speak the truth of Christ with loving zeal. Increase the number of people who will be doers of the word and not merely hearers deceiving themselves.

By every available medium send your saving word to the limits of human habitation that there may no longer be dark places unlit by the shining word of your grace in Jesus Christ.

We pray for our country and for our government, that justice may be fulfilled and that all citizens be led to contribute to the common good.

Hear our prayers for the sick and the sorrowing, especially those who have requested our supplications on their behalf or for one dear to them. Heal their injuries, cure their diseases, restore them to health and strength, that they may rejoice in your mercy.

Have compassion on those who in grief and bitterness eat ashes like bread and mingle tears with their drink. Lift up those who are depressed and others who have no sense of their own dignity in your sight. Bring peace of mind to the disturbed and freedom to the addicted.

God of creation, after six days of work you rested from your labor. Your people go out to their work and to their labor until the evening. After a lifetime of work also you give us retirement and then final rest from our labors.

We thank you for all those who once worked beside us but now have entered into the rest that you have prepared for the people of God. Grant us perseverance that we may complete the work you have for us to do here, and then receive us into heavenly service and rest, to the praise of your name, God most holy, God most loving, God most wise. Amen

Proper 12 (July 24-30)

First Lesson - Jacob works for Laban to obtain two wives, Leah and Rachel. Genesis 29:15-28

Psalm 105:1-11, 45*b*

Second Lesson - The Holy Spirit inspires our prayers in the bosom of God's family. Romans 8:26-39

Gospel - We hear more of the shorter parables of Jesus. Matthew 13:31-33, 44-52

CALL TO WORSHIP

Leader: The grace of our Lord Jesus Christ be with you all.
People: And also with you.
Leader: Give God thanks and invoke the hallowed name, making God's deeds known in the world around.
People: We will do this honor with song and psalm and think upon all of the wonders of God.

INVOCATION

We have gathered, O God, to hallow your name and ponder the wonders of your grace to us in Jesus Christ your Son. May the songs we sing in this sanctuary echo also in the places where we live and work on the other six days of the week; through Jesus Christ our Lord. Amen

PRAYER OF CONFESSION

Supreme Communicator, who can explain how you hear and speak to us? Divine-human Communication, how shall we properly acknowledge you as one who teaches and is the teaching? Internal Communicator, how can you be God and within us, unworthy and unknowing as we are? Yet we frequently live without adequate time set aside for prayer and meditation, smug in our small wisdom, self-satisfied and self righteous, though still so unlike your eldest Son, our Brother, Jesus. Forgive our misplaced values, for not treasuring your complete rule in us at the cost of all else. Our only hope is that you will continue to shape us in our life as your family with Jesus Christ. Amen

Declaration of Pardon

Pastor: Friends, hear the Good News! God knew his own before they ever were.

People: He calls us, justifies us, and gives us the splendor of the brothers and sisters of Jesus Christ.

Pastor: Friends, believe the Good News!

People: In Jesus Christ, we are forgiven.

[AND]

Exhortation

Cling to nothing as having any worth, besides the knowledge of the kingdom of heaven and the privilege of being a learner in it.

PRAYER OF THE DAY

Teller of parables, we need to learn in order to teach, but teach us by your tantalizing parables, that our imaginations may be stretched, and we will tell new parables as well as old ones. Amen

PRAYER OF THANKSGIVING

Hearer of prayers, Giver of wisdom, Advocate of God's people, we give thanks for every human leader who has sought and received your gifts, who has known and served you by whatever name. We thank you for patriarchs and matriarches, that you are the God of Sarah as well as of Abraham, of Rebecca as well as of Isaac, of Rachel as well as of Jacob. You make yourself known in days of pilgrimage as in years of exile and in periods of settlement. There is no place on earth where you cannot be worshiped and called upon, by whatever name or title, in any language, by people of many faults and faiths and differing customs. You deserve the thanksgiving of everyone everywhere, for you are God of all, responsive, generous, compassionate. Amen

PRAYER OF DEDICATION

How can we set a price on the parables of the kingdom or consider an admission charge to enter into your realm, Sovereign of sovereigns? Receive us, undeserving as we are, for the sake of our elder Brother, Jesus, Prince of peace, and sanctify these humble gifts by the Spirit's use. Amen

PRAYER OF INTERCESSION
AND COMMEMORATION

Founder of the church, hear your people as they pray for your church universal that it may be like a merchant in search of fine pearls for your pleasure. Better than earthly merchandise is what we can offer by invitation, as the prophet: Ho, everyone who thirsts, come to the waters; and you who have no money, come, buy and eat! Come, buy wine and milk without money and without price. May the church graciously offer your sacraments with generosity, that those who come to you may never be hungry and those who believe in you may never be thirsty or work again for the food that perishes, but for the food that endures for eternal life.

Creator and Sustainer of life, give your blessing to the earth that it may bring forth its increase abundantly and that farmers may gather in a great harvest and give us all reason for overflowing thanksgiving.

To your tender mercies and healing care we commend all who suffer, all who are sick, all who are hurt. Soothe the troubled, calm the anxious, cool the fevered, strengthen the weak. Grant wisdom and carefulness to all surgeons, physicians, nurses, ward attendants, and medical technicians that our hospitals and clinics may bring new health to many. Bless all pastors and chaplains who minister to the dying that their final days may be trustful and expectant of your mercy.

For we know that if the earthly tent we live in is destroyed, we have a building from God, a house not made with hands, eternal in the heavens. We give thanks for those already passed over into eternity and ask your saving grace that we may also enter your presence with great joy when our time comes. To you, our God, Parent, Brother, and Holy Spirit, be given all the glory, time without end. Amen

Proper 13 (July 31-August 6)

First Lesson - Jacob has a unique experience of God. Genesis 32:22-31

Psalm 17:1-7, 15

Second Lesson - Paul writes with anguish for the unbelief of his own kindred. Romans 9:1-5

Gospel - Jesus would rather feed people than turn them away. Matthew 14:13-21

CALL TO WORSHIP

Leader: The grace of our Lord Jesus Christ be with you all.

People: And also with you.

Leader: In the morning come to know God's true love.

People: This morning we put our trust in the gracious kindness of the eternal One.

INVOCATION

This morning and every morning we know your true love and provision for our daily needs, O God. This morning we join our voices in praise and prayer, publicly proclaiming our gratitude and invoking your continued care of us in body, mind, and spirit; through Jesus Christ our Lord. Amen

PRAYER OF CONFESSION

Unsparing God, pleading Christ, satisfying Spirit, we confess that we spend a lot of time and energy in the pursuit of what does not satisfy for long. We forget your promises and provisions and fall into times of depression and despair. We underestimate the extent of your love and the lavishness of your gifts. Forgive such doubt and ingratitude, and bring us to the overwhelming victory that is ours; through Jesus Christ who loved us and loves us still. Amen

Declaration of Pardon

Pastor: Friends, hear the Good News! Nothing in all creation can separate you from the love of God in Christ Jesus.

People: That's true: Nothing in all creation can separate us from the love of God in Christ Jesus our Lord.

Pastor: Friends, believe the Good News!

People: In Jesus Christ, we are forgiven.

[AND]

Exhortation

Share the bread of forgiveness and the cup of salvation with others who are hungry and thirsty for God's love.

PRAYER OF THE DAY

Feeder of multitudes, enable us to find the hidden resources in ourselves and our neighbors, to share the spiritual food of your loving words so that the hungry in spirit do not go away searching aimlessly for that which will satisfy to all eternity in the company of Jesus. Amen

PRAYER OF THANKSGIVING

Unstinting Giver, eternal Gift, embracing Spirit, your love can conquer in all ircumstances. You enable us to survive persecution with forgiving spirits. You give us patience to endure hardship. You grant us courage to face peril. Even death is overcome with resurrection. For such invaluable and imperishable gifts we are eternally grateful. Thanks be to you, O God, for your giving without stint. Thanks be to you, O Christ, for your death, resurrection, and advocacy. Thanks to you, family Spirit, for your unfailing love. Amen

PRAYER OF DEDICATION

No gifts of ours, divine Giver, can be equated with yours. Multiply our offerings of hand and heart to satisfy the spiritual and physical need of multitudes to the glory of your name. Amen

PRAYER OF INTERCESSION
AND COMMEMORATION

High and holy One who inhabits eternity, in Christ you have come down to those who are contrite and humble in spirit, to revive the spirit of the humble and to revive the heart of the contrite. Rejuvenate your people by the grace of the Holy Spirit so that your church may manifest more clearly your living presence with us. Refresh your people who are overworked and weary. Redirect any congregations that serve arrogantly and do not reflect your humble and suffering Son, Jesus Christ.

Bless all who have done us good, whether known to us or unknown, those who have helped us directly or who have remembered our needs before your throne of grace. If we are estranged from anyone, reconcile us by the forgiving Spirit, that all bitterness and hostility may be removed and the unity of the Spirit be manifest in the bond of peace. Deliver the innocent from temptations too hard for them to bear, and support those on the verge of losing faith and giving up the good fight. Have mercy on hardened sinners and those enslaved by grievous addictions. May these surrender to your higher power.

Send true comforters to those who are suffering from the malice of others or by the mistreatment of the careless; any who have been misjudged and misunderstood; and those who are victims of injustice and oppression because of their race, their religion, or their sex. Hasten the day of liberty and justice for all.

Be near, O Lord, to the sick and the suffering. Uphold all who are bearing pain and loss bravely, both the afflicted and those who care for them. Help them as they have need, and give them reason to rejoice in Christ our Savior.

We pray, Compassionate Christ, for your healing Spirit to assist psychiatrists, psychologists, counselors, and mental health workers who work with those who are mentally and emotionally ill. We are grateful for the good that some medicines can do and pray that further helpful treatments and cures may be discovered for their healing and care. We are filled with gratitude that the mentally handicapped and mentally ill can approach you with confidence and assurance of your loving care both now and in eternity.

By the grace of our Lord Jesus Christ, your love, O God, and the communion of the Holy Spirit, we are one with all your faithful people on earth and in heaven. We remember with thanksgiving all who have lived the Christian life before us and are now resting from the struggle and testing of life in the world. As they enjoy their repose with you, sustain us in our time of probation that we may be found faithful to enter into heaven and serve you with all saints and angels and bring glory to your holy name, Fatherly, Brotherly, Motherly God, time without end. Amen

Proper 14 (August 7-13)

First Lesson - Joseph's dreams are dangerous to his health. Genesis 37:1-4, 12-28

Psalm 105:1-6, 16-22, 45*b*

Second Lesson - Heartfelt faith in Christ confessed openly is the means of our salvation. Romans 10:5-15

Gospel - Jesus comes to his disciples in an unexpected way. Matthew 14:22-33

CALL TO WORSHIP

Leader: The grace of our Lord Jesus Christ be with you all.
People: And also with you.
Leader: Remember the many acts of God's faithful love.
People: We believe the promises of the eternal One and sing praises to God.

INVOCATION

Gracious God, we come to worship you, confessing our faith before others and confirming it in acts of affirmation. Hear our prayers and our praise through our risen Lord, Jesus Christ. Amen

PRAYER OF CONFESSION

God of all worlds, God of all weathers, God of all seasons, we confess that we often look and listen for you in the wrong place or with the wrong attitude. We are too easily moved by the many voices of denial rather than by the lonely voices of truth, too readily awed by the catastrophic and not by the quiet growth of the living, too drawn to the fire of enthusiasms, too repelled by the solitary duty you sometimes expect. Forgive the casual way we throw in the towel when the opposition grows too strong. Pardon the pride, the fear of failure, and the fear of death that prevent our full loyalty to the covenant you have made with us in Jesus Christ. Amen

Declaration of Pardon

Pastor: Friends, hear the Good News!

People: Deliverance is near to those who worship God.

Pastor: Friends, believe the Good News!

People: In Jesus Christ, we are forgiven.

[AND]

Exhortation

Take heart! Christ is with us in the Spirit. Do not be afraid. Go when he calls you. Have faith that he will not let you down.

PRAYER OF THE DAY

Son of God, in the midst of storm and strife, rough going and contrary winds, come to assure us of your power and purpose, that we may be saved to confess your name and be faithful in following you wherever you lead us. Amen

PRAYER OF THANKSGIVING

God of patriarchs and matriarchs, Messiah to the synagogue and Christ to the church, Holy Spirit enlightening our consciences, we are grateful for every experience of your presence and your help. We bless you for the history of your people Israel, for the covenant you made with them, for the Psalms and the promises, and for the patience you have had with them and with us. We listen for you still, in the company of worshiping people and in the solitude of our lonely prayers, to discern your voice and identify your directions for us to take. We rejoice with apostles and prophets and all faithful people who praise your goodness and follow you in the way of peace; through Jesus Christ our Lord. Amen

PRAYER OF DEDICATION

From the yields of the harvest and from the fruits of our labors, we bring you, supreme God, these offerings. Receive these signs of our fidelity in response to the measure of prosperity you have permitted us; through Jesus Christ our Lord. Amen

PRAYER OF INTERCESSION
AND COMMEMORATION

Holy Parent in heaven, your Son Jesus returned to you after praying for us who are still in the world. Protect us, as he prayed, because we belong to him. Grant us the unity for which he prayed, sanctifying us in the truth, celebrated with joy. As you sent Jesus Christ into the world, so send us into the world also, not in disarray but in the unity of the Spirit. Care for the newcomers who believe in Christ through the word of the gospel, that they may all be one in the body of Christ and that there may be no dissension within the body—that all the members, old and new, may have mutual care for one another.

Bless our country with prosperity and peace, with honest employment for all who can work, and a cooperative spirit that gives us peace in our common life. Deliver us from those who are troublemakers, self-seeking and trying to conquer by dividing us.

Compassionate Christ, teach us to serve you by befriending the neglected, the disoriented, the aged, and the lonely. You are the same, yesterday, today, and forever. By the Spirit be close to the sick who look to you for healing and help. Show your mercy to the dying whose hope is in the Risen Christ.

As your people Israel sought a homeland, so may we, with those who have already entered your presence, seek the way home with Jesus Christ. As you have received them, so also accept us who have been baptized in your holy names, Father, Son, and Holy Spirit, yours forever. Amen

Proper 15 (August 14-20)

First Lesson - Joseph forgoes vengeance for forgiveness and largesse. Genesis 45:1-15

Psalm 133:1-3

Second Lesson - Paul praises the wideness of God's mercy. Romans 11:1-2*a*, 29-32

Gospel - Jesus teaches that purity has more to do with the heart than with the hands, with the spirit than with the external. Matthew 15:10-28

CALL TO WORSHIP

Leader: The grace of our Lord Jesus Christ be with you all.
People: And also with you.
Leader: Mark my teaching, O my people, listen to the
      words I am to speak. I will tell you a story with

meaning, I will expound the riddle of things past, things that we have heard and known, and our parents have repeated to us.

People: We will mark your teaching and listen to the words you speak. We will hear a story with meaning that we have heard and known, and our parents have repeated to us.

INVOCATION

Self-revealing God, we have come to know more of you even in the contemplation of the stories we have heard before in our childhood. We come not only to hear your word but to seek the gifts of the Spirit to do your will; through Jesus Christ our Lord. Amen

PRAYER OF CONFESSION

God of all nations, your name is loved and hallowed in many languages. Yet nowhere in the world is your justice perfectly maintained and the right always done. We confess that we do not worship you in complete allegiance to your covenant with us nor in loving openness to all people of all nations, of all customs, of all conditions. We forget the mercy you have shown us in our time of disobedience, and we do not share your readiness to show mercy to those who are now disobedient. Forgive us for the sake of your all-loving Son, Jesus of Nazareth. Amen

Declaration of Pardon

Pastor: Friends, hear the Good News! Jesus Christ has made a covenant with us to take away our sins.

People: The gracious gifts of God and his calling are irrevocable.

Pastor: Friends, believe the Good News!

People: In Jesus Christ, we are forgiven.

[AND]

Exhortation

Show mercy as you have received mercy, for it is God's purpose to show mercy to all humanity.

PRAYER OF THE DAY

Son of David, Son of God, heal our souls, that we may be saved from our doubts and know the healing of faith that restores both us and those to whom you send us, of whatever nation or condition. Amen

PRAYER OF THANKSGIVING

God of farmers and fishermen, we thank you for the harvest of the sea and the land and for every wise plan of distribution that shares the plenty of the world with the greatest number of people, in this generation and those to come. God of all courts and legislatures, we are grateful for good laws and good decisions that overturn injustice and right wrongs, that protect the life of the vulnerable and restrain the power of the ruthless. God of all prophets and priests, we worship you whose face of truth and love we have seen in Jesus Christ. We rejoice in the spread of the good news in the world by word and deed, and celebrate your purpose to show mercy to all humankind. All praise be given to you, God of justice, God of salvation, God of mercy. Amen

PRAYER OF DEDICATION

May our offerings and our prayers, universal God, be so generous as to take in the needs of the whole world, and especially the hungry, that our aid may seem like manna from heaven to those who receive it, in the name of Jesus Christ. Amen

PRAYER OF INTERCESSION AND COMMEMORATION

May your gracious hand be upon us, O God, in all that we do from day to day and upon all who teach, those who write, those who make music, those who paint and sculp and make works of art, those who act, comedians and tragedians, those who do research and invent new tools and find new cures for our illnesses. Keep us from wasting our talents, and direct us in ways that are for the benefit rather than the detriment of society.

We pray for the continuance of religious freedom in our land, that not only the church but every religious group may be free to search for the truth that we have found in Jesus Christ. Forgive those who misuse your name and teach them reverence by the good example of others.

Safeguard the life of the weak and the vulnerable by the protection of honest and caring police who stand against the violent and rapacious. Preserve and perfect our best customs, and lead us back from the misuse of sex and drugs and the exploitation of the poor.

Comfort and relieve those who are sick and sorrowful, especially those who desire our prayers. Grant them patience as they wait upon you and an early and happy emergence from their hard times to better days.

You, O LORD, will keep our going out and our coming in from this time on and forevermore. Keep us is the way that leads to eternal life that we may rejoin those pilgrims who have walked with us as we journeyed with Christ and already have been received into the celestial city. Prepare us for the day when the trumpets sound for us on the other side. With all the hosts of heaven and all your congregations in the earth, we will give glory to your name, Fatherly, Brotherly, Motherly God. Amen

Proper 16 (August 21-27)

First Lesson - The baby Moses is spared the genocide planned by Pharaoh. Exodus 1:8-2:10

Psalm 124:1-8

Second Lesson - Paul calls the Romans to a more distinctive personal worship. Romans 12:1-8

Gospel - Simon Peter rises to prominence in his confession of faith in Jesus as the Christ. Matthew 16:13-20

CALL TO WORSHIP

Leader: The grace of our Lord Jesus Christ be with you all.
People: And also with you.
Leader: The judgements of God are unsearchable, but
    search them out.
**People: We will continue to plumb the depths of God's
    wisdom to trace the ways of divine providence.**

INVOCATION

Infinite God, our minds cannot comprehend you, but we are bidden by your Spirit to worship you in sincerity. Expand our knowledge of you that our trust may be deeper and our loyalty stronger; through Jesus Christ our Lord. Amen

PRAYER OF CONFESSION

Source, Guide and Goal of all that is, we acknowledge that though we come from you, we have not always followed the guidance you have given us in Jesus Christ. We have certainly not reached the goal of perfection that lies ahead of us. Do not leave unfinished the work you have begun in us. Though there is more to know about you than we can ever learn, we are often distracted from our search for the truth. Even when we have known Jesus to be the way, we have been diverted by less strenuous climbs. Though there are many awesome things in our world, we have not seen beyond them to revere you. Be patient with us for the sake of Jesus Christ, our elder and wiser brother. Amen

Declaration of Pardon

Pastor: Friends, hear the Good News! God's true love endures forever.

People: The Lord will accomplish his purposes for us.

Pastor: Friends, believe the Good News!

People: In Jesus Christ, we are forgiven.

[AND]

Exhortation

Let us confess in our own times that Jesus is the Messiah, the Son of the living God. This is no longer a secret to be locked up, but a door to be opened.

PRAYER OF THE DAY

Son of the living God, you have entrusted the keys of the kingdom not merely to Peter but to all who confess your name, for your promises are as wide as the heavens. Prevent us from closing what you want open and opening what you want closed, according to your wisdom and unfailing love. Amen

PRAYER OF THANKSGIVING

God of all generations, God of prophets and apostles, God of royalty and commoners, you are worshipped in tent and temple, in chapel and cathedral. Your great glory is sung by the simple and the wise, by poets and hymnists, by the untrained voice and the cultured singer. Your wisdom is sought by the illiterate and the widely-read, under the open heavens and in libraries and places of learning. We rejoice that, though you are beyond our grasp, you have come within our reach in Jesus of Nazareth. Though your ways are untraceable, we may come to you by the way of Jesus, your Son and the Son of Mary, to you be glory forever. Amen

PRAYER OF DEDICATION

Wise God, we can tell you only what you have taught us. Generous God, we can return to you only what you have already given us. Receive us and our gifts, for we have found our way to you through Jesus Christ. Amen

PRAYER OF INTERCESSION
AND COMMEMORATION

We entreat you, holy and loving God, to bless your church with leaders who are devout and humble in their obedience to you and caring in their oversight of your congregations. May your church walk warily in times of controversy, patiently when scorned by crowds, and boldly when the circumstance calls for leadership.

Add to the church converts from sin to holiness, from unbelief to faith, from uncertainty to a firm commitment to the Lord of the church, Jesus Christ. Increase the numbers of the younger generation who should follow us into the faithful service of the church as we are open to their youthful spirits and new ideas.

Parent of all parents, who has called us to be brothers and sisters of Jesus Christ in your heavenly family, bless our human families that they may be a school of faith and morality in preparing our children and ourselves for your service in society at large.

Hear our prayers for our own country and for all the nations of our world. Mediate our differences, ameliorate our privations, overrule our misuses of power, banish hatred and strife, and call all people to a love of justice and peace.

Creator and Healer, we are fearfully and wonderfully made. Wonderful are your works; that we know very well. We ask for your continued healing of our diseases, the mending of broken bones, the recovery of those who have had surgery, and the cure or control of disease and pain by medication.

Heal our minds and spirits by your word of truth and the sanctification of our spirits by your Holy Spirit. Comfort all who mourn and steady those who will soon experience death.

Eternal God, whose Son Jesus is the resurrection and the life. Assure all who believe in him that even though they die they will live. We remember with thanksgiving those most dear to us who have already passed through death into the life everlasting.

Since we are receiving a kingdom that cannot be shaken, let us give thanks and offer to you acceptable worship with reverence and awe and walk before you in godliness and with love for the whole company of your saints on earth and in heaven. To your name, Father, Son, and Holy Spirit, be all glory and praise, now and forever. Amen

Proper 17 (August 28-September 3)

First Lesson - Moses encounters God in a burning bush while tending sheep and is called to shepherd the people of Israel. Exodus 3:1-15

Psalm 105:1-6, 23-26, 45c

Second Lesson - Paul turns to specific moral admonitions that reflect the teaching of Jesus Christ. Romans 12:9-21

Gospel - Peter and the disciples have more to learn about the mission of Jesus as Messiah. Matthew 16:21-28

CALL TO WORSHIP

Leader: The grace of our Lord Jesus Christ be with you all.

People: And also with you.

Leader: Persist in prayer. Let love for our community breed warmth of mutual affection.

People: With unflagging energy, in ardor of spirit, we will serve the Lord.

INVOCATION

We come to you again, Holy God, in this holy place, to receive your view of things and to offer continued service to you as you call us to mission. Speak to us by whatever name you will authorize us to communicate, through the Spirit of Jesus Christ. Amen

9/01/02

PRAYER OF CONFESSION

~~Thoughtful~~ God, we confess that ~~our thoughts~~ we are too content with easy ways and the avoidance of suffering. ~~Though you anoint your people to the stresses of leadership, we prefer the safety of obscurity. You sanctify us as prayerful priests to intercede for the whole world.~~ Too often we pray only for ourselves and not for the nations around your globe. Forgive us for the sake of the cross- bearing Christ. Amen

Declaration of Pardon

Pastor: Friends, hear the Good News! The Lord will redeem us.

People: Our Lord Jesus will show us his favor.

Pastor: Friends, believe the Good News!

People: In Jesus Christ, we are forgiven.

[AND]

Exhortation

Adapt yourselves no longer to the pattern of this present world, but let your minds be remade and your whole nature

167

thus be transformed. Then you will be able to discern the will of God.

PRAYER OF THE DAY

8/28/05

God of the gospel, Leader of disciples, Spirit of divinity and humanity, plant the cross in our hearts, that our worldly selfishness may die and our true self be raised from death to heavenward life. Amen

PRAYER OF THANKSGIVING

Faith-giving God, body-shaping Christ, nature-transforming Spirit, we love the beauty of the body of Christ being transformed from the uncoordinated movements of worldly behavior to the choreography of obedience to your will. We listen with eagerness to gifted voices that speak your gracious word. We work enthusiastically with others who also seek to serve you and who call out the best gifts we have been given. We worship you with mind and body, as in Jesus Christ you have revealed your grace in his mind and body. We believe; we will obey; we are being changed thanks to you, loving God. Amen

PRAYER OF DEDICATION

Uniting Christ, gather the varied personal gifts we bring into a functioning body with grace and accomplishments acceptable to you. Amen

PRAYER OF INTERCESSION AND COMMEMORATION

Powerful God, you have given us as head of the church your Son holy and true, Jesus Christ, who has the key of David, who opens and no one will shut, who shuts and no one opens. May all your people seek to follow him through the doors of opportunity that are open to us in our own times and leave behind projects and programs that are no longer useful. Preserve your church everywhere in patient endurance to any opposition to your word, and keep us from the hour of trial that is coming on the whole world to test the inhabitants of the earth.

Encourage all Christians in every land to hold fast to what has been given them, that their crown of glory may not be taken away but, having overcome, they may stand before you as pillars in the temple of God and bear the name of your heavenly city, and your own new name, O Christ of God.

Heavenly Parent, we commend to you all who are joined to us by ties of family and affection, especially the little children dear to us and the aged who have become like children again. Guide us in our changing relationships as our children mature to adulthood and we adjust to a new interdependence as time requires. Make us all rich in the Spirit, reverent toward you and loving one another as we love ourselves.

Renew to health and strength those who are sick, those who are recovering from illness or accident, surgery or other treatment. Comfort the mourners and give peace to the dying. Eternal God, you remember that we are dust, mortals whose days are like grass, flourishing like a flower of the field: the wind passes over it, and it is gone, and its place knows it no more. But your steadfast love is from everlasting to everlasting on those who fear you, and your righteousness to children's children, to those who keep your covenant and remember to do your commandments. Your throne is in the heavens, and your kingdom rules over all. Bring us from faithful service in this world to more intimate service in heaven with all who now serve you in heaven as they did less perfectly in earth, through Jesus Christ to whom, with you and the Holy Spirit, be glory and praise, time without end. Amen

Proper 18 (September 4-10)

First Lesson - The passover is planned and prepared in readiness for the exodus of the people of Israel from slavery in Egypt. Exodus 12:1-14

Psalm 149:1-9

Second Lesson - Paul's moral admonitions are a bridge from the Old Testament to the New. Romans 13:8-14

Gospel - Jesus outlines ways to reconcile differences between members of the church. Matthew 18:15-20

CALL TO WORSHIP

Leader: The grace of our Lord Jesus Christ be with you all.

People: And also with you.

Leader: Be assured that the Lord is here. For Jesus said, "where two or three are gathered together in my name, I am there among them."

People: We are assured that the Lord is here. Our Risen Lord is here among us.

INVOCATION

We praise you, O God, in the assembly of the faithful, singing to you a new song as well as old songs, for we are glad to be your people and the children of your royal house. Receive us as we worship in the Spirit of Jesus Christ. Amen

PRAYER OF CONFESSION

Demanding God, loving God, holy God, we find it difficult to live up to your expectations. You make loving our neighbor an inescapable duty. We would rather be selective about our relationships and limit our responsibilities to those with whom we have a natural affinity. We do not like being corrected by others and do not like to appear judgemental when we correct others. Is it only prophets and rulers whom you call to be sentinels of the moral security of the nation? Do you hold us all accountable if we do not speak out against evil? Forgive our silence if you have prodded us to speak in your name, through Jesus Christ, Son of Mary, Son of God. Amen

Declaration of Pardon

Pastor: Friends, hear the Good News! The Lord will be good to his servants, as he has promised.

People: The Lord will be good to us, as he has promised.

Pastor: Friends, believe the Good News!

People: In Jesus Christ, we are forgiven.

[AND]

Exhortation

Be under obligation to no one—the only obligation you have is to love one another.

PRAYER OF THE DAY

Heavenly Parent, Brother of sinners, Spirit in the church, help us to agree in our prayers and in our common life, that your purposes may be accomplished, your will obeyed, and your children reconciled to each other and gathered to Christ in the church. Amen

PRAYER OF THANKSGIVING

God of order, God of grace, God of the people, we are grateful for the commandments you have given to order our common life. We appreciate the teaching of Jesus as to how we are to interpret and implement them. In seeking to be reconciled with those who have sinned against us and with those against whom we have sinned, we are thankful for the aid of the Spirit. Grant that our happiness may always be in obedience to your commandants, in loving our neighbors as our-

171

selves and loving you above all. We would be your obedient servants and loving children, a happy people gathering around the living Lord. Amen

PRAYER OF DEDICATION

Lord of the church, receive our offerings as an expression of our love for you and for one another, that we may continue to gather here in your presence to hear your word and to pray together. Amen

PRAYER OF INTERCESSION
AND COMMEMORATION

Your hand, O God, is gracious to all who seek you, but your power and your wrath are against all who forsake you. Overrule and overthrow tyrants who ignore your rule and who exploit others by violence or drug addiction or sexual abuse. Stiffen the resistance to evil of good people in governments and religious institutions, especially that your justice may be exercised through them as well as your mercy.

We pray for your church that members everywhere be serious and discipline themselves for the sake of their ministry of intercession. May your congregations be hospitable to one another, maintaining constant love for one another, for love covers a multitude of sins. Remind your people that, notwithstanding your grace and mercy, all will have to give an accounting to you, who are ready to judge the living and the dead. So may we all learn to live in the Spirit as you do.

Recall to your church those who have gone astray or neglected the assembly of your people. Reconcile those who have quit the church through dissension or prideful controversy. Renew your church in finding new approaches to those outside the church, that adaptability may be an evidence of grace to grow and change for the sake of others. Preserve the best of the past in the present and in our future adapted to changing times.

Bless our physicians, for their gift of healing comes from you, the Most High. May their skills be sharpened and appreciated by their patients. Bless those whose research is finding and developing new medicines that you have created with the elements of the earth. Save us from fanatics who despise the gifts you have given to doctors and pharmacists and other therapists.

Sustain self-help groups that serve individuals who need to give up addictive drugs and harmful diets. Cleanse hearts from all sin that healing may proceed from a spirit made whole and dependent on you, their higher power. You have created us as body, mind, and spirit and can make us whole persons in communion with you and with one another.

Good Shepherd and Kindly Light, you have safely led many of our relatives and friends as sheep through the dark valley of the shadow of death into the security and glory of your heavenly fold. Bring us at the last to them and to you in rest and peace everlasting, through our Savior, Jesus Christ, to whom—with you, our Parent, and the Holy Spirit—be all praise and honor. Amen

Proper 19 (September 11-17)

First Lesson - The Israelites get safely through the sea but the water returns to cover the pursuing Egyptian army. Exodus 14:19-31

Exodus 15:1*b*-11, 20-21

Second Lesson - Paul admonishes the Romans to forego judgment of one another since in the end God will judge us all. Romans 14:1-12

Gospel - Jesus makes it clear that we are not to expect forgiveness from God if we can not forgive one another. Matthew 18:21-35

CALL TO WORSHIP

Pastor: The grace of our Lord Jesus Christ be with you all.

People: And also with you.

Pastor: Keep our Lord Jesus in mind as you honor the first day of the week.

People: We will keep our Lord Jesus in mind as we honor the day of his resurrection.

INVOCATION

Gracious God, we honor you and extol your power in raising Jesus from death to life eternal. Receive us patiently, for our worship is not worthy of you. We approach you through your faithful son Jesus and in his name. Amen

PRAYER OF CONFESSION

Father-in-heaven, Brother-in-heaven, Mothering Spirit-everywhere, we confess that we try your patience with our inconsistencies. We expect you to forgive our grossest sins, but are unwilling to forgive the petty sins of our brothers and sisters, our neighbors and friends. We recount for those closest to us the number of times they have offended us, but forget the numberless times you have forgiven us for a wide range of sins. We want justice for our neighbor's misdemeanors, but mercy for our own felonies. We do not have the same tolerance for others as we have for ourselves. Forgive such unevenness, merciful God. Amen

Declaration of Pardon

Pastor: Friends, hear the Good News! God pardons our guilt and surrounds us with constant love.

People: God pardons our guilt and surrounds us with tender affection.

Pastor: Friends, believe the Good News!

People: In Jesus Christ, we are forgiven.

174

[AND]

Exhortation

Since God has not treated us as our sins deserve nor requited us for our misdeeds, let us be forgiving, not only seven times, but seventy times seven.

PRAYER OF THE DAY

Holy Ruler, suffering Prince, saving Sovereign, persist in your dealings with us until we have learned to forgive as you forgive and to love our neighbors as we love ourselves, that your realm may be extended from heaven to earth. Amen

PRAYER OF THANKSGIVING

Universal God, from Greenwich to Greenwich, from pole to pole, you are our God, and there is no other, There is no place where we can escape your justice, but also no place where your mercy does not reach. No journey into space can take us beyond the bounds of your love. There are limits to our understanding of your ways in human history, and endless questions, but your patience and love fill us with gratitude and praise. Glory to God in the highest. Glory to God on earth. Glory to God in the church. Amen

PRAYER OF DEDICATION

Let these offerings, divine Employer, be a sign of our service, that we do not live and do not work for ourselves alone, that whether we live or die we are yours. Amen

PRAYER OF INTERCESSION AND COMMEMORATION

Hear us, O God, as we intercede in the name of Christ for all humanity.

Give to your church a deeper insight and a wider outlook so that the eternal message of Jesus Christ, not confused with any human tradition, may be heard as good news in every generation with new life for the world. Sustain your church whether in hostile or peaceful circumstances so that vows of membership may be kept loyally and your sacraments received with joy. Everywhere may your people bear patiently the reproach of unbelievers and witness humbly of their trust in Jesus Christ as Lord.

Invisible Sovereign, grant to every nation a new sense of relationship in your one family. May human rights everywhere spring from faith in one God who made us male and female like God's Self. May all nations unite in restoring order where there has been natural disaster and rebuilding what has been laid waste by war or other human violence. Save us from the worship of firepower and destruction to respect for ministries of healing and rebuilding and improving living standards for all.

In your tender mercy, O Christ, enfold the sick, the suffering, and the bereaved. May your joy be their strength.

Let quietness and confidence in you, with whatever treatment human medicine can afford, heal their spirits as well as their bodies.

Creator and preserver of things eternal, save from destruction what we do in the power of your Spirit, and redeem us from the service of what rusts and decays. Teach us how to lose our lives for your sake that we may find them again made perfect with all your saints in heaven.

All our prayers we offer in the name of Jesus Christ, to whom with you, O God, and your Holy Spirit be all glory and praise now and forever. Amen

Proper 20 (September 18-24)

First Lesson - When the Israelites complain of hunger to Moses and Aaron, God sends bread from heaven. Exodus 16:2-15

Psalm 105:1-6, 37-45

Second Lesson - Paul shares with the Philippians the conflict between keeping on or being relieved by death from present suffering. Philippians 1:21-30

Gospel - Jesus suggests that those of us at this late hour of the Christian day may still be rewarded for our work as if we had been there at the beginning. Matthew 20:1-16

CALL TO WORSHIP

Leader: The grace of our Lord Jesus Christ be with you all.

People: And also with you.

Leader: Add joy to your faith. Be one in spirit and one in mind.

People: We will joyfully stand firm as we contend for the gospel faith.

INVOCATION

We draw near to you, Generous God, not just with complaints and petitions but with praise and contrition. Hear our prayers and our hymns as from the heart we make our boast in Jesus Christ. Amen

PRAYER OF CONFESSION

Owner of land and sea, Ruler of wind and wave, Spirit of Jesus Christ available to your people, we confess that we grumble about the work you give us to do when it seems that we work longer and get no more reward than those have not worked as long and hard. We have not always found joy in our work for its own sake nor rejoiced in what others have done, whether early or late. In the silence of this place we acknowledge your right to do whatever you will with what is yours, but when our work and our life is tedious, we complain uncivilly. Forgive our disrespect for you and our disregard for the task you have given us to do. With the help of the Spirit we may yet learn to find joy in your service. Amen

Declaration of Pardon

Pastor: Friends, hear the Good News! Even when we do not remember God's acts of faithful love,

People: our Savior delivers us for his name's sake.

Pastor: Friends, believe the Good News!

People: In Jesus Christ, we are forgiven.

[AND]

Exhortation

Add joy to your faith and let your conduct be worthy of the gospel of Jesus Christ.

PRAYER OF THE DAY

Heavenly Sovereign, save us from the jealousy that seeks to detract from the accomplishments of others, especially the young and those who have come late in life to your service, that all of us working together may find joy in serving you as one body, one in Spirit, one in mind. Amen

PRAYER OF THANKSGIVING

Who can count, gracious God, the times you have relented from destroying rebellious and stubborn people forgetful of your past mercies and turning to idolatry, the worship of lesser things? How often has a Moses thrown himself into the breach to save a nation? How grateful we are that your special child, Jesus, has done this for the whole world. We rejoice that whether we have come early or late to work for Christ in the church, you reward us beyond our deserving. Thanks be given to you, gracious God, mediating Christ, reconciling Spirit. Amen

PRAYER OF DEDICATION

Patient God, may our offerings never be given as an excuse for indulgence after we have completed our Sunday service, but rather as a portion that signified our discipline in worship and daily life, in the name of Jesus Christ. Amen

PRAYER OF INTERCESSION
AND COMMEMORATION

God Most High, make your universal church as a city that is bound firmly together, a new Jerusalem, your holy habitation. Send your Spirit as a river whose streams make glad the city of God so that glorious things are spoken of you, O city of God.

Spare your church from self-willed opinion, which tends to the subversion of the faith and unity of the church. Save your church from intransigence, an unwillingness to broaden the scope of what the Holy Spirit may teach us with more light from the Holy Scripture.

Hear our prayers for our country. May your church be an embodiment of your truth for our times, a letter of Christ, written not with ink but with the Spirit of the living God, not on tablets of stone but on tablets of human hearts. So strengthen the moral fiber of our nation, leaders and people alike. Make us strong to do your will in the family of nations.

If we are affluent, let us not set our hopes on the uncertainty of riches but rather on you who richly provides us with everything for our enjoyment. Whether rich or poor may we choose to share ill- treatment with the people of God rather than to enjoy the fleeting pleasures of sin. When we are doing well, may we not forget the less fortunate; may we bear one another's burdens and in this way fulfill the law of Christ.

As the apostles gave the name Barnabas (which means "son of encouragement") to a Levite of Cyprus, Joseph, so may we be people of encouragement, speaking to other people for their upbuilding and encouragement and consolation. Save us from being overly judgmental and squelching what may be the work of the Holy Spirit in a form that is new to us.

We remember before you those who are distressed in body, mind, or spirit, especially those known and dear to us, whom we name in our hearts. Bless not only doctors and nurses and professional caregivers, but the visitation of your people that they may bring a healing presence of your Spirit.

We remember before you with thanksgiving our dear departed family and friends. As you have led them safely through the valley of the shadow of death into green pastures and beside still waters, so bring us at last to such tranquility, beyond all trouble and sorrow, temptation and failure.

And to you, Fatherly, Brotherly, Motherly God, we will attribute all unconditional love and grace. Amen

Proper 21 (September 25-October 1)

First Lesson - A miracle is required for God to provide water in the wilderness for the thirsty Israelites. Exodus 17:1-7

Psalm 78:1-4, 12-16

Second Lesson - Paul gives the Philippians the prime example of genuine humility that all of us require. Philippians 2:1-13

Gospel - Jesus uses some provocative language and a parable in replying to the chief priests and elders of the people. Matthew 21:23-32

CALL TO WORSHIP

Leader: The grace of our Lord Jesus Christ be with you all.

People: And also with you.

Leader: Exalt our Sovereign God, and extol God's name,
the One who is holy and mighty.

**People: We will extol the One who is holy and mighty,
who loves justice and forgives our misdeeds.**

INVOCATION

Glorious are your deeds, O God, and we proclaim them in
our own generation and to generations following us. You
speak to us in great mysteries and in common daily gifts.
Primarily, we know you and come to you through Jesus
Christ, in whose preeminent name we pray. Amen

PRAYER OF CONFESSION

God who is, God who acts, God who moves others to act, you
are righteous, principled in all you do, considerate in all you
seek to accomplish with others. Our sins give evidence of the
evil that is still a part of our nature. Our actions are often
unprincipled, based on self-interest, and showing little concern for the rights and feelings of others. We make promises
we have no intention of keeping, simply evading an honest
declaration of our priorities and commitments. We make
excuses that are transparent to almost everyone but ourselves. We are ashamed to acknowledge our vanity and rivalry with others. Forgive our inordinate pride, our
undependable word, our uncertain service, for the sake of
your humble, dependable, and obedient servant and Son,
Jesus the Christ. Amen

Declaration of Pardon

Pastor: Friends, hear the Good News! God will hold innocent all who seek forgiveness of their misdeeds.

181

**People: God holds us innocent because we seek forgive-
ness of our misdeeds.**

Pastor: Friends, believe the Good News!

People: In Jesus Christ, we are forgiven.

[AND]

Exhortation

Have the same love to one another. Look to each other's
interests and not merely to your own. Have the same turn of
mind and common care for unity like Jesus Christ.

PRAYER OF THE DAY

Deliver us, gracious Savior, from the delusion that only scan-
dalous sinners need to repent and believe, so that by acknowledging our imperfections, we may change our minds, and
by believing more deeply, obey you more consistently. Amen

PRAYER OF THANKSGIVING

Exalted Parent, humble and exalted Brother, shared Spirit, we
rejoice in the story of Jesus of Nazareth. We revel in the
mystery of his equality with you, which he willingly abandoned to work as a slave to serve humanity's needs, to die as
a criminal to free us from our sins, to rise to glory and the
exaltation of a name that is more glorious than any other
name. We praise you in the world's greatest music and in the
simplest words of children. Receive our humble worship and
sincere praise today and always. Amen

PRAYER OF DEDICATION

No service of ours is too humble to offer to you, suffering
Servant, who, having served in earthly humility, has returned to the place of heavenly honor. We offer you the best
we can do. Amen

PRAYER OF INTERCESSION
AND COMMEMORATION

Majestic God, may your presence in the church be widely acknowledged as your people grow from strength to strength, from truth to truth, from loving to loving. Without your Spirit we are lifeless and barren. As we abide in Christ the vine, we bear much fruit to the glory of your name.

Bless all who invest themselves in your work through the church, visiting the sick and aged, teaching classes, maintaining the property, keeping accounts and paying the bills, making music, and doing committee work.

Especially bless those who have left homeland and family to take your gospel to where it has not been heard. Strengthen the church where it is an overwhelmed minority surrounded by people of other faiths or of no faith. May your strength be evident in their weakness.

Sovereign above all earthly leaders, hear our prayers for our country and all our elected officials that we may be led in ways of truth and justice. Bless the members of the United Nations, that increasingly ways of negotiation and peace-making may defuse explosive conflicts between nations, races, and religions.

Hear our prayers for all who, after they have escaped the defilements of the world through the knowledge of our Lord and Savior Jesus Christ, are again entangled in them and overpowered, their present state becoming worse for them than the first. Deliver them by your powerful hand as they turn in desperation to you again. God of hope, fill them with all joy and peace in believing so that they may abound in hope by the power of the Holy Spirit.

Hear our prayers for those who are passing through times of anxiety, sleepless, restless, not knowing what to do. Grant them peace of mind as they put their trust in your daily care and keeping. Heal the sick, strengthen the weak, comfort the sorrowful, send friends to the lonely.

How precious is your steadfast love, O God! All people may take refuge in the shadow of your wings. In life and in death may we not be divided. We rejoice that you have received into heaven the faithful known and dear to us and we trust your mercy to accept us as well, for the sake of Jesus Christ, the source of our life in Christ Jesus, who became for us wisdom and righteousness and sanctification and redemption.

O the depth of your riches and wisdom and knowledge, O God! How unsearchable are your judgments and how inscrutable your ways! To you, Fatherly, Brotherly, Motherly God we give all honor and thanksgiving, time without end. Amen

Proper 22 (October 2-8)

First Lesson - Here are recorded ten great commandments to govern our relationship with God and our neighbors. Exodus 20:1-4, 7-9, 12-20

Psalm 19:1-14

Second Lesson - Paul finds his new life as a Christian to be much more valuable than his previous life and career. Philippians 3:4b-14

Gospel - In this parable Jesus sets his whole mission in death and resurrection as a conundrum for his opposition to ponder. Matthew 21:33-46

CALL TO WORSHIP

Leader: The grace of our Lord Jesus Christ be with you all.
People: And also with you.
Leader: Invoke the God of the gospel by name.
People: Our Creator and Redeemer will grant us new life in the Spirit.

INVOCATION

God of covenant, God in Christ, God in communion with us, we come to worship because we have heard the good news of Jesus your Son and have accepted the new covenant in his blood. Speak your word to us again today through the Spirit of Jesus Christ. Amen

PRAYER OF CONFESSION

God of Israel, God of the Church, God of all worlds, you gather your people in order to cultivate in them the fruits of justice and goodness. Too often we neglect our relationships in the community, so that it looks like an untended vineyard. We do not sense the decline of faith and the loss of virtue that comes without the pruning disciplines of self-examination through the hearing of your word of judgment and salvation. Forgive our laxity that results in lack of spiritual fruitfulness that we should manifest in Jesus Christ. Amen

Declaration of Pardon

Pastor: Friends, hear the Good News! God calls us to the life above in Christ Jesus.

People: We hear God's call to the life above in Christ Jesus.

Pastor: Friends, believe the Good News!

People: In Jesus Christ, we are forgiven.

[AND]

Exhortation

Forget what is behind you and reach out to that which lies ahead, the goal and the prize of heavenly glory in Christ Jesus.

PRAYER OF THE DAY

Cornerstone of the Church, remind us of who you are, that we may never reject you and your claims for our reverence and obedience, made known by prophets and apostles, who

185

with us are built into an abiding structure for your service among the nations. Amen

PRAYER OF THANKSGIVING

God of the many and the few, God of the weak and the strong, God of saints and sinners, we celebrate your patient care of your people in all times and places. We rejoice in your continuing patience with your people Israel. We are grateful for the broad inclusiveness of the church of your Son, Jesus. How rich is the spiritual heritage you have passed on to us through Judaism and the Christian church! How challenging is the honorable task you have given us to pass it on! Be near always to hear our thanksgiving with our prayers and petitions; through Jesus Christ our Lord. Amen

PRAYER OF DEDICATION

Divine Sovereign, receive from us what is your due, not only these tokens from our hands but the worship of our hearts and the obedience of our daily lives and work, after the example of Jesus of Nazareth. Amen

PRAYER OF INTERCESSION
AND COMMEMORATION

We seek you, O God, and make supplication to you not only for ourselves but our neighbors, whom you have commanded us to love as we love ourselves. Hear our intercession in the name of Jesus Christ, who loved us and gave himself for us that he might redeem us from all iniquity and purify for himself a people of his own who are zealous for good deeds.

To this end, revitalize your church and every mission to serve the world, which you so loved that you gave your only Son, so that everyone who believes in him may not perish but may have eternal life. May we be your eyes to see human need, your ears to hear cries for help, your hands to gently touch and support the weak, your feet to go wherever we are needed. Keep your church strong to do your will on earth as it is done in heaven.

As we leave our gifts and offer our prayers before your altar, O God, grant that first we may be reconciled to our brothers and sisters, that our offerings and intercessions may be sincere and worthy of your hearing. We commend to your keeping all those dear to us by ties of blood and the unity of the Spirit. Give your angels charge over them to guard them in all their ways.

Compassionate Christ, give rest to those who are weary and are carrying heavy burdens. Cool the fevered brow, heal the sick, mend the broken body or spirit, deliver those in trouble, forgive the sinning who look to you for grace.

We praise you, O Lord, with all our hearts and voices and bless your holy name, for you have saved us from destruction and rescued us in time of trouble. For this reason we thank you and praise you and bless your name not only for our own salvation but the safekeeping of our loved ones who have passed through the hazards of this life to the peace of heaven. Lead us through the narrow gate that opens to life eternal. We will worship and glorify you with all the company of the faithful in heaven and earth. Amen

Proper 23 (October 9-15)

First Lesson - Aaron and the people succumb to idolatry in the absence of Moses, who is communing with God on the mountain. Exodus 32:1-14

Psalm 106:1-6, 19-23

Second Lesson - Paul urges the Philippians not to get bogged down in petty quarrels but to find joy in the appreciation of good qualities in people and in themselves. Philippians 4:1-9

Gospel - Jesus continues speaking in parables to stimulate human readiness for divine judgement. Matthew 22:1-14

CALL TO WORSHIP

Leader: The grace of our Lord Jesus Christ be with you all.

People: And also with you.

Leader: My friends, all that is true, all that is noble, all that is just and pure, fill your thoughts with these things.

People: All that is lovable and gracious, whatever is excellent and admirable, will fill our thoughts.

INVOCATION

We turn from the thought of lesser things to ponder your greatness, O God. Make yourself known to us again through the words of Holy Scripture, the hymns we sing, the prayers we say, the creeds we confess to believe. We worship you worthily only through Jesus Christ our Savior. Amen

PRAYER OF CONFESSION

Universal Sovereign, Universal Prince, Universal Spirit, you provide us spiritual riches in great abundance. You are rightly insulted by our indifference to your invitation to celebrate the union of Christ and the church. We are undeserving of your gracious invitation and often scandalized that you would accept others we consider even less deserving. Forgive the rude treatment that we have given your emissaries and our indifferent preparedness when we do heed your invitation. Grant us time to reconsider our priorities, to push aside more mundane things, and in giving place to your rule, to escape the judgement that would otherwise await us. God, have mercy on us; Christ, have mercy; Holy Spirit, be merciful to us. Amen

Declaration of Pardon

Pastor: Friends, hear the Good News! The peace of God, which is beyond our understanding, will keep guard over your hearts and thoughts, in Christ Jesus.

People: The peace of God, which is beyond our understanding, will keep guard over our hearts and our thoughts, in Christ Jesus.

Pastor: Friends, believe the Good News!

People: In Jesus Christ, we are forgiven.

[AND]

Exhortation

Put into practice all that you have received from the Christian tradition: what you have heard and what you have seen done by the Christians who have set an example for you.

PRAYER OF THE DAY

Attending Spirit, prepare us for fellowship with the Son of heaven and our royal Parent, so that, clothed in the beauty of holiness, we may enjoy the heavenly feast that celebrates the victory of Christ over sin and death. Amen

PRAYER OF THANKSGIVING

God of Moses and of Miriam, his sister, you are worshiped not only in psalms but in tambourine and dance, for you free the enslaved and bring them out to freedom. Christ Jesus, founder of the church, we rejoice that the names of all who struggle in the cause of the gospel are in the roll of the living. Timeless Spirit, you bring together into one people those who fight at Sinai and Philippi. We rejoice that you can make community of those who have been in conflict, both in the process of time and the climax of history. Your name, O God, endures forever. Amen

PRAYER OF DEDICATION

As we stand in your house, O God, we present these tokens of our servanthood. We would serve you both in worship and in the cause of human justice with Jesus Christ, who practices what he preaches. Amen

PRAYER OF INTERCESSION AND COMMEMORATION

Gracious God, may your grace continue to overflow for all your people with the faith and love that are in Christ Jesus.

May our intercessions rise before you like incense, like the prayers of the saints in heaven along with the perfect prayers of our advocate with you, Jesus Christ the righteous.

With him we pray that your kingdom may come and your will be done, on earth as it is in heaven. Strengthen your whole church to serve you faithfully in the world. May the obedience of your people in Christ, members of his body, serve to call others to obedience and membership in the church. May your people continue to heed the word of Jesus to cure the sick and say to them, 'The kingdom of God has come near to you.' As a mother comforts her child, so may your healing Spirit bring calm to those who are disturbed and direction to those who are lost. Strengthen those who have lived indulgently to take up the cross and follow Christ in the selfless service of others.

Bless all who care for the sick in homes, hospitals, nursing homes, and hospices. Send them not only cures for the body but balm for the soul, new physical wholeness and more mature spiritual life.

Eternal God, we rejoice in the faith that you have received out of our sight not only your Son Jesus in his ascension but also many of our comrades in the way of the cross. Keep us faithful and true to you all the days of our journey, that we may arrive at last at your heavenly house in peace and ready for the rest you have prepared for your weary pilgrims;

through Jesus Christ our Lord, who, with you and the Holy Spirit, is worthy of all glory and honor, time without end. Amen

Proper 24 (October 16-22)

First Lesson - Moses experiences as much of the divine glory as is possible and permissable. Exodus 33:12-23

Psalm 99:1-9

Second Lesson - Paul gives thanks for the faith of the young church in Thessalonica. 1 Thessalonians 1:1-10

Gospel - In response to a loaded question from his adversaries, Jesus gives a pithy proverb to guide us in dividing our loyalties to God and country. Matthew 22:15-22

CALL TO WORSHIP

Leader: The grace of our Lord Jesus Christ be with you all.
People: And also with you.
Leader: Put no faith in princes but in the Creator, who also watches over the stranger and gives heart to the orphan and widow.
People: We will trust our Creator who watches over us.

INVOCATION

By coming to your house of prayer, Gracious God, we show that our faith is in you above all others. Receive our worship as we extol your greatness and your compassionate care for all your people; through Jesus Christ our Lord. Amen

PRAYER OF CONFESSION

Creator of heaven and earth, Maker of all humanity, Judge of all persons, hear our confession. Though we worship you now we frequently show more respect for powerful political figures than for you. We are more concerned about the bills we owe to the tax collector and the business people than what we owe to you and your church, both in money and in personal service. Though you have made us in your likeness, we behave as if we are self-made and with no obligation to please you, our Maker, and no duty to serve you, our Teacher, and no accountability to you, our Judge. Forgive our false claims to what is yours and our ungrateful use and abuse of your creation; for the sake of Jesus Christ, our Savior. Amen

Declaration of Pardon

Pastor: Friends, hear the Good News! Brothers and sisters beloved by God, receive the divine gifts of grace and peace.

People: We are brothers and sisters beloved by God, who has chosen us and sent the Good News to us.

Pastor: Friends, believe the Good News!

People: In Jesus Christ, we are forgiven.

[AND]

Exhortation

Show your faith in action, your love in labor, and your hope in courage. Live in the power of the Holy Spirit, with strong conviction.

PRAYER OF THE DAY

Sovereign above all sovereigns, clarify our vision of your majesty, that all worldly powers may appear in proper proportion to your authority, and duly order our allegiances, so that we may give you and our neighbor what is due, in the Spirit of Jesus Christ. Amen

PRAYER OF THANKSGIVING

Living and true God, we praise your name and give thanks for all who have spread faith in your name. We rejoice in the victory of Jesus over death and in our deliverance from the terrors of judgment to come. We celebrate the persuasive power of the Spirit to strengthen our convictions and enable our service. We are grateful for all the ties of love and friendship that cross tribal lines and language barriers, recovering the unity of the human family. With the whole brotherhood and sisterhood of Jesus Christ, we praise you, Paternal, Fraternal, Maternal God. Amen

PRAYER OF DEDICATION

Empowering Spirit, strengthen our convictions, that we may always give God what is due to God and to governments what is due to governments and to your church what is due to your church; through Jesus Christ our Lord. Amen

PRAYER OF INTERCESSION
AND COMMEMORATION

God of peace, give your church prophets who will speak to people for their upbuilding and encouragement and consola-tion. Spare the church from self-appointed critics who delight in tearing down and ripping apart. May your loving Spirit teach each of us how to please our fellow members in the church for the good purpose of building them up. Let us as a denomination pursue what makes for peace and for mutual upbuilding.

We pray for those who serve on the frontiers of the church, who, like the apostle Paul, make frequent journeys, in danger by boat or car or plane, in danger of violence from bandits, in danger from strangers. Watch over and keep them, whatever their ministry in the name of Christ: preaching, teaching, healing, translating, or publishing and distributing the scriptures.

In city and suburb, in country and wilderness, send your people to gladden the solitary and bring glad tidings of good things to those in despair.

The gift of healing comes from you, Most High, and we pray that this endowment may not be abused but serve to restore the sick and bring thanksgiving not only to the healer but to you. May all who administer our health systems know themselves to be good stewards of the many skills and tools of medicine, remembering that they will give account like all of us for the best use of time and talent.

Holy and forgiving God, we rejoice in the answer of your Son Jesus when he was entreated by the sinner, "Jesus, remember me when you come into your kingdom." May all who are near death hear his reply, "Today you will be with me in Paradise." And as you have fulfilled this promise to many of our predecessors in the faith, so fulfill it for us as well when our time comes to pass over from this life. We will honor your name in life and in death, life-giving Parent, up-rising Jesus, ever loving Spirit, One God. Amen

Proper 25 (October 23-29)

First Lesson - With the death of Moses, Joshua succeeds to his the leadership of the people of Israel. Deuteronomy 34:1-12

Psalm 90:1-6, 13-17

Second Lesson - Paul expresses a motherly affection for the church at Thessalonica. 1 Thessalonians 2:1-8

Gospel - Jesus asks questions, as well as answering them, in a debate with the Pharisees. Matthew 22:34-46

CALL TO WORSHIP

Leader: The grace of our Lord Jesus Christ be with you all.

People: And also with you.

Leader: Revere our Sovereign God. There are many blessings in store for those who honor God and do the will of our Sovereign.

People: We will honor God and do the will of our heavenly Sovereign.

INVOCATION

God of power, love, and truth, bless us as we hallow your name in our prayers and our praise, both in the hour of public worship and in our daily lives. Grant us to know the undergirding of the Holy Spirit as we will to do your will; through Jesus Christ our Lord. Amen

PRAYER OF CONFESSION

God of high places, God of low places, God of all places, we confess that we are not full of compassion as you are. We are prone to forget what it is like to be aliens, to be powerless, to be vulnerable, to be without an advocate, to be without credit. Forgive our complicity in heartless systems that make credit cheap and easy for those who need it least and prohibitive for those who need it most. Forgive indifference toward, or ill-treatment of, widows and orphans when we forget that they could be our own widows and orphans. We need to repent of all our less-than-loving behavior and attitudes for the sake of your all-loving Son, Jesus of Nazareth. Amen

Declaration of Pardon

Pastor: Friends, hear the Good News! God has approved us as fit to be entrusted with the Gospel.

People: God has approved us as fit to be entrusted with the Gospel.

195

Pastor: Friends, believe the Good News!
People: In Jesus Christ, we are forgiven.

[AND]

Exhortation

Love our Sovereign God with all your heart and soul and mind and your neighbor as yourself.

PRAYER OF THE DAY

Loving God, captivate our emotions in the worship of you, integrate our personhood in communion with you, and make us wise in the knowledge of you, that we may love ourselves truly and our neighbor in the same way, like our loving brother, Jesus Christ. Amen

PRAYER OF THANKSGIVING

God of strength and gentleness, we rejoice in the gentleness we see in those who care fondly for children. We are grateful for the deliberate beneficence of those who have more than they need and provide for those who are needy. We are thankful for those who use their power not to exploit others but to defend and protect those who are vulnerable to exploitation. We are glad to honor all who declare the good news of Jesus Christ without base motives of greed or hunger for power. Help us always to seek only your favor and to pass every test of our motives in serving others, as did Jesus Christ, our example. Amen

PRAYER OF DEDICATION

Receive, our gifts and ourselves, sovereign God, so that we may be faithful envoys of the good news and the witness of our church be fruitful with your help. Amen

PRAYER OF INTERCESSION
AND COMMEMORATION

Mighty God, to our supplications and thanksgivings and other prayers, we add our intercessions for everyone in the name of Christ our Savior.

May your hand be with your church, O Lord, here and everywhere, that others may become believers and turn to you. May all church members remain faithful to you with steadfast devotion, full of the Holy Spirit and of faith. Make us worthy to be called "Christians." Like the early church, may we support the church according to our ability, sharing our resources and sending relief where it is direly needed.

Christ our king, your kingdom is an everlasting kingdom. Extend your dominion through all generations in all places. You are faithful in all your words and gracious in all your deeds. Not only in our nation but in all countries of the world, may your word be heard and obeyed, your gracious Spirit be honored, and your works of love carried out.

Most gracious God, in Christ you have become our Savior; no messenger or angel, but your presence saves us. You lift up and carry those without strength. In your love and pity restore to health and strength those who are sick and suffering. Be present to those who are close to death, that they may be reassured of your grace with strong hope to pass beyond seeing you now in a mirror, dimly, but afterwards to see you face to face, knowing fully what now they know only in part.

Eternal God, gladden our hearts in days of grief and loss with the remembrance of your promises of ultimate wholeness after death by your final saving act. When we remember those whose company we miss, remind us that they are beyond all sin and sorrow, and sustain us in our hope to be with them when our earthly life is ended. To Jesus your faithful witness, to you our heavenly Parent, and to your loving Holy Spirit be ascribed all honor and glory, time without end. Amen

Proper 26 (October 30-November 5)

First Lesson - Joshua leads the people of Israel through the Jordan River to the promised land. Joshua 3:7-17

Psalm 107:1-7

Second Lesson - Paul also uses a masculine analogy to explain his fatherly discipline of the church in Thessalonica. 1 Thessalonians 2:9-13

Gospel - Jesus chides the Pharisees for not practicing what they preach. Matthew 23:1-12

CALL TO WORSHIP

Leader: The grace of our Lord Jesus Christ be with you all.

People: And also with you.

Leader: Receive God's message, not as the word of men, but as what it truly is, the very word of God at work in you who hold the faith.

People: We receive God's message, not as the word of human beings, but as the very word of God at work in us who hold the faith.

INVOCATION

Through the written and spoken words of fallible human beings, your Spirit, O God, brings us your very word of truth and grace revealed to our humanity in Jesus Christ your Son. We have gathered to hear more of that saving word and to express our gratitude to you in the name of Jesus. Amen

PRAYER OF CONFESSION

Heavenly Parent, strong as any father, gentle as any mother, we are dependent on you for both life and sustenance. Forgive our moments of pride when we act as if we did not need you. Rabbi above all other rabbis, Teacher above all teachers, forgive us if at times we act like know-it-alls, unteachable and dogmatic about what we do and do not believe. Leader, anointed One, forgive any move we make to displace you, whether in exalting ourselves in places of authority or in giving to others the honor due only to you. Be patient with us, as a parent dealing with immature children, for the sake of your mature child, Jesus Christ. Amen

Declaration of Pardon

Pastor: Friends, hear the Good News! Those who humble themselves will be exalted.

People: We who are humble before God will be exalted.

Pastor: Friends, believe the Good News!

People: In Jesus Christ, we are forgiven.

[AND]

Exhortation

Achieve true greatness. Be a willing servant of those around you who are your brothers and sisters.

PRAYER OF THE DAY

By your words and by your lifestyle, teach us Rabbi-Messiah to speak your word graciously and to serve others humbly, that we may not exalt ourselves only to be brought low by your judgment. Amen

PRAYER OF THANKSGIVING

Gracious God, we thank you for your call to enter into your kingdom and glory. We are grateful that your living word is at work in us to prepare us for worthy service in your realm. We express our thanksgiving for the advice and encouragement of our fathers and mothers and our brothers and sisters in the faith and all who have imparted to us your good news. We will show our gratitude by committing ourselves to others in the same kind of caring ministry, sharing your loving word, through Jesus Christ our Lord. Amen

PRAYER OF DEDICATION

O God, help us to give and live, worthy of the call into your realm of glory, through Jesus Christ our Lord. Amen

PRAYER OF INTERCESSION
AND COMMEMORATION

Our God, you are good to all, and your compassion is over all that you have made. Your universal Spirit prompts our prayers for all that you have made, both animate and inanimate.

Preserve your creation with the dedication of human ecologists guiding us in our stewardship of the good world that you have made and that continually needs to be gardened with your guidance and blessing. Help us undo whatever we may have done that has ravaged the land, that it may be restored for the enjoyment of generations yet unborn.

Sustain your church in every generation. Give wisdom to parents and teachers who hand down to children the tradition of the biblical revelation preserved from the beginning of the church. May your church always be open to new truth coming out of your word. Give the ignorant a hunger for wisdom, the doubting a desire for firm faith, the disloyal a will to return to the faith, the tempted a victory over evil, the enslaved freedom from addiction, and the despairing hope in our Risen Lord. Guide those who have not found their vocation in life, that they may recognize and use their best gifts for the common good.

As in the spring the bloom of the first crocus gives us hope of the end of winter, so grant a sign of better days to those in days of discouragement and in the dry land of grief. Grant that their present wilderness and desert shall rejoice and blossom with new life. Send your healing Spirit to treat the sick and encourage those who care for them.

Grant to all your people, in poverty or wealth, in sickness or health, in weakness or strength, in life or in death, the confidence that nothing, past, present, or future, can separate them from your love, which is in Christ Jesus our Lord.

And now we thankfully commemorate before you our wise and godly ancestors who have followed Christ through death to glory. Keep us in unbroken communion with them by the Holy Spirit, who enables our prayers and our daily obedience to your commandments. To you, Fatherly, Brotherly, Motherly God, we ascribe all majesty, dominion, and gracious power, time without end. Amen

All Saints (November 1 or First Sunday in November)

First Lesson - The prophet celebrates the conquest of death still to come. Isaiah 25:6-9

[OR]

The wise one celebrates the immortality of the righteous in the care of the Eternal One. Wisdom of Solomon 3:1-9

Psalm 24

Second Lesson - John foresees an immortality that is rich with a loving personal relationship to God. Revelation 21:1-6

Gospel - The death of Lazarus is the occasion for a miracle of Jesus and a promise of eternal life for all who would come after him. John 11:32-44

CALL TO WORSHIP

Leader: The grace of our Lord Jesus Christ be with you all.
People: And also with you.

Leader: God has spoken. Be glad and rejoice.
People: We will be glad and rejoice in the salvation of God.

INVOCATION

Eternal God, whose beginning is beyond our knowing and whose life is unending, we come to worship because you have made yourself known to us in Jesus Christ. We are filled with wonder that in his incarnation he accepted mortality in order to provide for our immortality. We pray to you through his Living and Holy Spirit within us, in the name of Jesus our Lord. Amen

PRAYER OF CONFESSION

Eternal God, nothing is more awesome for us than death, which we know to be inevitable but which we cannot fully understand. We often question the timeliness of death, wondering if it is really occasioned by your plan or only the result of natural causes. Forgive any doubts that we may have that the resurrection of Jesus Christ holds promise for us and all your people as well. In his name we pray. Amen

Declaration of Pardon

Pastor: Friends, hear the Good News! Grace and mercy are upon the chosen in Christ.

People: The faithful will abide with God in love.

Pastor: Friends, believe the Good News!

People: In Jesus Christ, we are forgiven.

[AND]

Exhortation

Trust in God, and you will understand all the truth you need on this side of the grave and have strong hope of eternity with God.

PRAYER OF THE DAY

Jesus, Lord of life and death, free us from the fears that bind us and help us to live a day at a time, trusting that you will provide for us what we need and in the end will take us to the place you have gone to prepare for us. Amen

PRAYER OF THANKSGIVING

God our savior, Christ our pioneer, Eternal Spirit, we give hearty thanks for our hopes of life everlasting. Your prophets foresee banquets and other signs of your abounding grace. Your word promises the intimacy of personal caring and the wiping away of the last of our tears. Who can fully imagine the glories prepared by the Risen Christ for those who will be received through his grace? All glory be given to you the Alpha and the Omega, the beginning and the end, the Creator of life, and our final Home. Amen

PRAYER OF DEDICATION

God invisible, God incarnate, God inspiring, the offerings we bring to our Lord's table are simple signs of our hope for the great feast you prepare in heaven. Receive these gifts and the offering of ourselves as living sacrifices acceptable to you through Jesus Christ our Lord. Amen

PRAYER OF INTERCESSION AND COMMEMORATION

Abba, Father, your Son Jesus taught us to pray with such familiarity and also most profoundly to pray for the coming of your kingdom on earth.

Teach the rich the blessedness of generosity and the poor the enjoyment of what they have with thanksgiving, and provide for them what they cannot live without. Teach us all to share unselfishly, that there may be enough of your good gifts of the earth for all.

Grant to our leaders in government a concern for people, that they may seek to provide for others the benefits they take for themselves. Teach us all to do to others as we would have them do to us.

Discipline our reactions to hostility so that our response to violence may be restrained and that both our private life and our public life may be more orderly and peaceful.

Bless every program that seeks to provide for the hungry both in emergency situations and where famine is endemic. May we share both surpluses of food and skills to help the hungry raise more food for themselves.

Be with your church everywhere, but especially we remember Christian minorities that are persecuted for their faith by people and governments committed to another faith. Grant them consolations in their suffering and grace sufficient for their needs.

We rejoice in your promise that the holy ones of the Most High shall receive the kingdom and possess the kingdom forever and ever. We celebrate the communion of your people on heaven and earth and hope for the day when your will may be done on earth as it is in heaven. Bring us all into one holy company, no longer separated from each other by any distance or dimension or disagreement that we may gather to worship you, Father, Brother, Mother, in one holy family forever. Amen

Proper 27 (November 6-12)

First Lesson - Joshua must reiterate the insistence of Yaweh to be worshiped solely and not as just one among many gods. Joshua 24:1-3*a*, 14-25

Psalm 78:1-7

Second Lesson - Paul reaffirms his faith that there is to be either personal resurrection or ascension for us as for Jesus. 1 Thessalonians 4:13-18

Gospel - Jesus tells a parable about ten bridesmaids, five of whom were wise and five foolish. Matthew 25:1-13

CALL TO WORSHIP

Leader: The grace of our Lord Jesus Christ be with you all.
People: And also with you.
Leader: Offer to God the sacrifice of thanksgiving.
People: We will pay our vows to the Most High.

INVOCATION

God Eternal, Son of God, mortal and immortal, Living Spirit, we are gathered to worship you and to encourage one another with words of scripture and spiritual songs and collective prayers. Receive our renewed pledges of fidelity to you and the church of your beloved Son: in his name. Amen

PRAYER OF CONFESSION

God of the unchanging and the unexpected, we are hard put to know what the day of the Lord is, let alone when it may come. Much of life seems cyclical, going around and around and not moving in any perceptible direction. Justice seems less like a flowing river and more like a fountain that occasionally rises to great heights, only to subside again. Forgive us if we are more curious than concerned, more puzzled than prepared for your judgments whenever they come. Prepare us for the day of Christ's coming, in our death or in human history. Amen

Declaration of Pardon

Pastor: Friends, hear the Good News! Believe that Jesus died and rose again; and so it will be for those who died as Christians.
People: We believe that Jesus died and rose again; and so God will bring us back to life with Jesus.

Pastor: Friends, believe the Good News!
People: In Jesus Christ, we are forgiven.

[AND]

Exhortation

Keep awake in the spirit for you never know when the day or hour of the Lord will come.

PRAYER OF THE DAY

Ruler of heaven, grant us prudence in our preparation for your coming, that we may know what gifts of the Spirit are needed if we are to be ready to greet you with confidence and rejoicing. Amen

PRAYER OF THANKSGIVING

God the unchanging and the unexpected, we are grateful for constants in nature on which we can usually depend. We are thankful also for the unexpected that wakes us to the reality of your expectations. We appreciate the warning that comes in times of danger or sickness or accident, that remind us of our mortality and our need to be prepared for the kingdom still to come. May all the beauties and bounties of the natural world create in us a longing for the beauty and bounty of the eternal realm to which you bring all who look for it, through Jesus Christ. Amen

PRAYER OF DEDICATION

Self-sufficient God, there is nothing we can bring to you that you need, for all is already yours. You have come to our rescue again and again, so we merely honor you by these tokens of appreciation, through Jesus Christ our Lord. Amen

PRAYER OF INTERCESSION
AND COMMEMORATION

Hear, O God, the intercessions we offer on behalf of others.

You have wondrously kept alive the light of your church in the darkness of the world. May we, like the wise virgins, welcome the coming of the bridegroom with lamps trimmed and burning bright, well furnished by the Holy Spirit, the perpetual fire of truth and grace. For the world lies in darkness, and its inhabitants are without light. Let the light of Christ so shine in the church that those outside may come into that light.

Bless those in government who are committed to you. May their good example and integrity improve government morality and enable justice and peace to flourish in our land and in our world neighborhood.

God of compassion, you lift up the downtrodden and cast the wicked to the ground. Strengthen and support every ministry to the underprivileged. Give power to judges and agencies of justice, that the wicked may be subdued and the opportunity for repentance may be granted them.

We are bound to pray for those most dear to us who are in need of healing for a sickness, relief from suffering, joy for sorrow, or an end to days of trouble. Be their salvation and their peace.

We look with gratitude to the holy place you have created in heaven for those who love you and have been received by you. Though they are beyond the curtain in your temple, they are safe from all evil and suffering. As we gather around your table of the new covenant, may we be reminded of Christ's provision for us and renew our hope in the final feast we will enjoy with him and all our loved ones departed this life.

These our prayers we offer to you in the name of Jesus Christ, who lives and reigns with you and the Holy Spirit, for time without end. Amen

Proper 28 (November 13-19)

First Lesson - Deborah is a prophetess in Israel's tradition of male prophets. Judges 4:1-7

Psalm 123:1-4

Second Lesson - Paul urges moral alertness in view of the uncertainty of the time of the reappearance of Jesus Christ. 1 Thessalonians 5:1- 11

Gospel - Jesus tells us that our responsibilities are in proportion to our opportunities. Matthew 25:14-30

CALL TO WORSHIP

Leader: The grace of our Lord Jesus Christ be with you all.

People: And also with you.

Leader: Make vows to our Sovereign God and pay them
duly.

People: We will bring our tribute to the heavenly Monarch.

INVOCATION

No tribute we can bring is worthy of your majesty, O God, but we have come to pledge again our loyalty to your service. We can serve you commendably only in the Spirit as we are serious in our commitment to you; through Jesus Christ our Lord. Amen

PRAYER OF CONFESSION

God of fire and fury, God of mercy and salvation, who can stand in your presence when you are angry? You may rightly give sentence out of heaven, declaring judgement on kings and queens, on nobility as well as commoners. And yet you send prophets and apostles with words of warning, that we may repent of our sins and, turning from them, find mercy and salvation. Forgive our waste of time and of opportunities to improve our readiness for the coming of our Savior, Jesus Christ. Amen

Declaration of Pardon

Pastor: Friends, hear the Good News! God has not ordained us to the terror of judgment but to the full attainment of salvation through our Lord Jesus Christ.

People: We rejoice that God has not ordained us to the terror of judgment but to salvation through our Lord Jesus Christ.

Pastor: Friends, believe the Good News!

People: In Jesus Christ, we are forgiven.

[AND]

Exhortation

Hearten one another and fortify one another in the faith that we live in company with Jesus Christ.

PRAYER OF THE DAY

Divine Executive, remind us of our obligations to you so that we will not waste opportunities to use to the advantage of heaven the assets you have given us and be found empty-handed in the end. Amen

PRAYER OF THANKSGIVING

God of creativity, we acknowledge with wonder the gifts and talents you have given to human beings. What magnificent works of music have been composed and performed by many in centuries of productivity! What beautiful sanctuaries have been built to the glory of your name! What proliferations of hospitals and other institutions of healing have been raised by your inspiration! The unnumbered varieties of great works in writing and learning, on tapestry and canvas, are returns on the gifts you have given. We thank you for the opportunity of serving you with whatever talents we have and ask that you receive them by the grace of our Lord Jesus Christ. Amen

PRAYER OF DEDICATION

Sovereign God, you are properly honored with the tributes of the great and the small, by the famous and the unknown. Receive what we offer as tokens of our faithful use of whatever talents you have given us, to the honor of your name. Amen

PRAYER OF INTERCESSION AND COMMEMORATION

Creator God, from one ancestor you made all nations to inhabit the whole earth and allotted the times of their existence and the boundaries of the places where they would live. Though the people of the world live within many boundaries of earth, we are from you and from one stock. You call us to pray for the whole human family to which you sent your Son, Jesus in death and resurrection, in humility and ultimate glory. Fulfill the purposes you set for us all and guide our prayers that they may not be at cross purposes with your will.

Raise up in every generation faithful messengers to speak your word to the partial truths and dangerous heresies that arise in every time in history. Expose false messiahs whose self-worship should be a warning to the credulous.

Save your people from political tyrants who forget that they are accountable to you for the powers that they have and abuse. May all live with respect for the judgment that will come, in assurance of your mercy to the repentant and severity for the intransigent.

God of our patriarchs and matriarchs, bless our land with honest leaders who seek your wisdom. Break down the barriers of race and religion and political partisanship.

Save us from deceit and false accusation, from greed and conspiracy, from indolence and overwork. Teach us the meaning of temperance in all things. Prosper our industry and bless our homes and families.

Hear our prayers for the sad and sorrowful; for the sick, whatever their disease; for the overburdened and the anxious; for the weak and the aged. Minister to each as they have need and as you know best.

Help us to count our blessings that this exercise may give us reason for thanksgiving and a basis for sharing them with others. Give us your compassion and concern for others.

Eternal God, we give thanks for the good memories we have of our godly dead who have completed their days on earth and have entered into the dominion of the immortal. Lead us in the paths of peace that will bring us at last with them into your immediate presence to worship you worthily in the Spirit to whom with you and our Savior Jesus Christ, be given all glory and thanksgiving. Amen

Christ the King - Proper 29 (November 20-26)

First Lesson - The great Shepherd to come, says the prophet, will care for the lean sheep pushed aside by the fat ones. Ezekiel 34:11-16, 20-24

Psalm 100

Second Lesson - The apostle rejoices in the faith of this congregation but prays for further growth toward maturity. Ephesians 1:15-23

Gospel - Jesus tells a parable of final judgement. Matthew 25:31-46

CALL TO WORSHIP

Leader: The grace of our Lord Jesus Christ be with you all.

People: And also with you.

Leader: Holiness is the beauty of God's temple while time shall last.

People: We worship God in the sanctity and freedom from our sins which Christ gives us through his life's blood.

INVOCATION

You are holy, God our heavenly Parent. You are holy, Jesus, our heavenly/earthly brother. You are holy, Spirit of God in the church. As we worship you, consecrate us by your purifying Spirit that we may become your holy children. Amen

PRAYER OF CONFESSION

Ancient in years, first-born from the dead, timeless Spirit, we confess that too often we are overawed by the wealth and power of human rulers, forgetting that they are as mortal as we are and that only Jesus Christ has won an impressive victory over death. Forgive us if political and national loyalties have superseded the dignity you offer us as a royal house of priests to serve you. You have sent us your faithful son Jesus Christ, but we listen to him less attentively than to less demanding voices around us. We admit that we too are among the people whose sins have wounded him. Forgive and free us from all our sins by the giving of his life's blood. Amen

Declaration of Pardon

Pastor: Friends, hear the Good News! The Christ loves us and freed us from our sins with his life's blood.

People: The Christ makes us a royal house to serve as priests of his God and Father.

Pastor: Friends, believe the Good News!
People: In Jesus Christ, we are forgiven.

[AND]

Exhortation

Look for the one who is coming with the clouds! Call to repentance all who have offended him.

PRAYER OF THE DAY

Sovereign of all, who is and who was and who is to come, raise us above the tides of natural events, and the ebb and flow of history, so that we may glimpse the glory of your eternal realm and be satisfied with no lesser honor than to serve you as witness to the truth in the company of Jesus Christ. Amen

PRAYER OF THANKSGIVING

Your majesty, eternal God, precedes and exceeds the grandeur of the seas, and your throne, unlike the passing dynasties of nations, does not pass away. Your truth, Sovereign over all earthly rulers, is full of grace and peace and not full of empty threatening so typical of the tyrants of our world. We join with the Seven Spirits before your throne in extolling you, the Alpha and the Omega, who is and who was and who is to come. May our thanksgiving continue not only while we have life and breath but through such coming generations as shall live until all people and nations of every language shall serve you. Amen

PRAYER OF DEDICATION

Our greatest gifts, Sovereign Creator, may not be given with pride because none can be worthy of your majesty. Receive them as token tributes to you signifying our humble service in the royal priesthood of all believers, through Jesus Christ, our Princely Priest. Amen

PRAYER OF INTERCESSION AND COMMEMORATION

God of all continents, as we celebrate thanksgiving again this week in our land of plenty, we pray for those who live in lands of draught and famine. Bless all who are undertaking to feed these starving people. Grant speed and safety to all who fly the big cargo planes laden with food raised by the farmers of our fertile lands.

As we pray for the success of the emergency feeding program we remember also the need for long-term solutions to the problems of hunger throughout our world. Break down the barriers of indifference that allow the people of the world's cities to ignore the plight of those who, out of sight, are out of mind. Inspire scientists in the exploration of problems of drought and the need for local solutions to land use and productivity. Help us to utilize new cosmic views from space to solve such problems as we get new perspectives on our global village.

We pray for Peace Corps volunteers and agricultural missionaries who have gone to share knowledge and experience with less developed countries and peoples. Give them skill in teaching and demonstrating the practices that have improved our diets and health in this bountiful country.

Although we enjoy the bounty and variety of the harvest, teach us to avoid waste, that we may have more to share with others in need anywhere in the world.

Hear our prayers for family and friends who are sick, anxious about uncertain diagnoses, impatient for a cure, or longing for relief from pain. Bless us all whatever the nature of our need. Comfort those who are dying.

You are the Alpha and the Omega, O God, who is and who was and who is to come. Our hope is in you because of Jesus Christ, the faithful witness, the firstborn of the dead, and the ruler of the kings of the earth. He loves us and frees us from our sins by his blood and makes us to be a kingdom, priests serving you. We are grateful for those known and dear to us who already serve before your throne. May your grace and peace enable us to serve you here until you call us to higher service. To you, God and Father of our Lord Jesus Christ, and to the Son and to the Holy Spirit be glory and dominion forever and ever. Amen

Scripture Index

Genesis

1:1–2:4	118
2:15-17, 3:1-7	66
6:11-22	121
12:1-4a	69
12:1-9	125
18:1-15 (21:1-7)	128
21:8-21	132
22:1-14	135
24:34-38, 42-49, 58-67	138
25:19-34	142
28:10-19	145
29:15-28	149
32:22-31	152
37:1-4, 12-28	156
45:1-15	159

Exodus

1:8-2:10	163
3:1-15	166
12:1-9	125
12:1-14	170
14:19-31	173
15:1b-11, 20-21	173
16:2-15	177
17:1-7	180
19:3-6	73
20:1-4, 7-9, 12-20	184
24:12-18	61
32:1-14	187
33:12-23	191

Leviticus

19:1-2, 9-18	58

Numbers

11:24-30	112

Deuteronomy

30:15-20	54
34:1-12	194

Joshua

3:7-17	198
24:1-3a, 14-25	204

Judges

4:1-7	208

1 Samuel

16:1-13	76

2 Samuel

7:1-11, 16	20

Psalms

2:1-12	61
8:1-9	118
13	135
15:1-5	47
16	91
17:1-7,15	152
19:1-14	184
23	98
23:1-6	76
24	201
27:1, 4-9	44
29:1-11	36
31:1-5, 15-16	102
31:9-16	82
32	66
33:1-12	125
40:1-11	39
45:10-17	138
46	121
66:8-20	105
68:1-10,32-35	109
72:1-7, 18-19	12
78:1-4, 12-16	180
78:1-7	204
80:1-7,17-19	9
86:1-10, 16-17	132
89:1-4, 19-26	20

Psalms

90:1-6, 13-17	194
95	73
96	24
99:1-9	61, 191
100	211
104:1a, 24-34, 35b	112
105:1-6, 23-26, 45c	166
105:1-6, 37-45	177
105:1-11,45b	149
105:1-6,16-22, 45b	156
106:1-6, 19-23	187
107:1-7	198
112: 1-9 (10)	50
116:1-4, 12-19	95, 128
118:1-2, 14-24	82, 88
119:1-8	54
119:33-40	58
119:105-112	142
121:1-8	69
123:1-4	208
124:1-8	163
126	16
130:1-8	79
133:1-3	159
139:1-12, 23-24	145
147:12-20	31
148	27
149:1-9	170

Isaiah

9:1-4	44
9:2-7	24
25:6-9	201
40:1-11	12
42:1-9	36
49:1-7	39
50:4-9a	82
58:1-9a (9b-12)	50
61:1-4, 8-11	16
63:7-9	27
64:1-9	9

Jeremiah

31:1-6	88
31:7-14	31

Ezekiel

34:11-16, 20-24	211
37:1-14	79

Micah

6:1-8	47

Wisdom of Solomon

3:1-9	201
10:15-21	31

Sirach

15:15-20	54
24:1-12	31

Matthew

2:13-23	27
3:13-17	36
4:1-11	66
4:12-23	44
5:1-12	47
5:13-20	50
5:21-37	54
5:38-48	58
7:21-29	122
9:9-13, 18-26	125
9:35-10:23	129
10:24-39	132
10:40-42	135
11:16-19, 25-30	138
13:1-9, 18-23	142
13:24-30, 36-43	145
13:31-33, 44-52	149
14:13-21	152
14:22-33	156
15:10-28	159
16:13-20	163
16:21-28	166
17:1-9	61
18:15-20	170

Matthew

18:21-35	173
20:1-16	177
21:1-11	83
21:23-32	180
21:33-46	184
22:1-14	188
22:15-22	191
22:34-46	194
23:1-12	198
25:1-13	205
25:14-30	208
25:31-46	211
26:14–27:66	83
28:1-10	88
28:16-20	118

Mark

1:1-8	13
13:24-37	9

Luke

1:26-38	20
1:46b-55	16
1:47-55	20
2:1-14 (15-20)	24
24:13-35	95
27:11-54	83

John

1:(1-9) 10-18	31
1:6-8, 19-28	16
1:29-42	39
3:1-17	69
4:5-42	73
7:37-39	112
9:1-41	76
10:1-10	98
11:1-45	80
11:32-44	201
14:1-14	102
14:15-21	105
17:1-11	109

John

20:1-18	88
20:19-31	92

Acts

1:6-14	109
2:14a, 22-32	91
2:14a, 36-41	95
2:1-21	112
2:42-47	98
7:55-60	102
10:34-43	88
17:22-31	105

Romans

1:16-17, 3:22b-28 (29-31)	121
4:1-5, 13-17	69
4:13-25	125
5:1-8	128
5:1-11	73
5:12-19	66
6:1-11	132
6:12-23	135
7:15-25	138
8:1-11	142
8:6-11	79
8:12-25	145
8:26-39	149
9:1-5	152
10:5-15	156
11:1-2a, 29-32	159
12:1-8	163
12:9-21	166
13:8-14	170
14:1-12	173
16:25-27	20

1 Corinthians

1:1-9	39
1:3-9	9
1:10-18	44
1:18-31	47
2:1-12 (13-16)	50

SCRIPTURE INDEX

1 Corinthians

3:1-9	54
3:10-11, 16-23	58
12:3-13	112

2 Corinthians

13:11-13	118

Ephesians

1:3-14	31
1:15-23	211
5:8-14	76

Colossians

3:1-4	88

Philippians

1:21-30	177
2:1-13	180
2:5-11	83
3:4b-14	184
4:1-9	187

1 Thessalonians

1:1-10	191
2:1-8	194
2:9-13	198
4:13-18	204

1 Thessalonians

5:1-11	208
5:16-24	16

Titus

2:11-14	24

Hebrews

2:10-18	27

1 Peter

1:3-9	92
1:17-21	95
2:2-10	102
2:19-25	98
3:13-22	105
4:12-14, 5:6-11	109

2 Peter

1:16-21	61
3:8-15a	12

Revelation

21:1-6	201

219